THE SALT OF THE EARTH

CAROL ROBINSON'S COLLECTED WORKS
BOOK SIX

THE SALT
OF THE
EARTH

The *Lone Star Catholic* Articles
(1958–1959)

Foreword by *Rodger Phillips*

AROUCA
PRESS

ISBN: 978-1-990685-89-7 (pbk)
ISBN: 978-1-990685-90-3 (hc)

Arouca Press
PO Box 55003
Bridgeport PO
Waterloo, ON N2J 0A5
Canada
www.aroucapress.com
Send inquiries to info@aroucapress.com

CONTENTS

PUBLISHER'S NOTE

THIS BOOK COMPRISES ALL OF THE KNOWN articles Carol Robinson wrote for *The Lone Star Catholic* which was the official newspaper for the Diocese of Austin, Texas. The founding editor was Dale Francis (1917-1992), a former Methodist pastor and convert to the Catholic Faith, who had a distinguished career in journalism. He was a good friend of Carol Robinson and she was invited to write a column which she did for a year from April 1958 to April 1959.

It was through my abiding interest and curiosity in all things related to Carol Robinson and the founding of her own magazine, *Integrity* (1946-1956) that I found a dissertation from 1965 on the short-lived *The Sun Herald*, a Catholic daily in Kansas City, itself influenced by many of the contributors to *Integrity*, and in which Carol Robinson was mentioned as having written for *The Lone Star Catholic*.

The articles found in this book were written several years after Carol Robinson's intense pursuit of a vision as seen in the pages of *Integrity*. It was a vision at odds with much of the mainstream Catholic view of society. It was radical, it challenged, it was uncompromising, and it gave voice to the frustrations of the laity who were trying to live a Catholic life in an un-Catholic world.

Written as short columns, she does not penetrate topics as deeply as in her *Integrity* articles but she continues her incisive critique of the modern world in this collection.

Her articles were written on the eve of the Second Vatican Council and I think she was hopeful that the Catholic Church would one day gain prominence as a force for good in the United States.

I hope this book further cements her reputation as one of the great American Catholic thinkers of the past hundred years. Hyperbole? Perhaps. However, I challenge every reader to seriously ponder her words written as they were with a heart and mind aflame with the truth of the Catholic Faith.

FOREWORD

I DISCOVERED THE AUTHOR CAROL JACKSON Robinson through her books. Not, at first, through the books she wrote. Rather her personal collection of books.

Carol lived in a 1725 saltbox Colonial in the Connecticut town of Redding, not far from New York City where her husband Maurice had worked for NBC. There in the antique farmhouse on Umpawaug Hill, she worked, and gardened, and wrote books and articles including the articles collected herein.

She was wed to Maurice and attended Mass at a small white gothic church, Sacred Heart, in the nearby village of Georgetown. After the institution of the Novus Ordo Mass in the 1970's the sacred space in the interior of the church was dismantled. Sumptuous tapestries were pulled down, statues were removed and paintings were covered over. During this stark, iconoclastic time Carol interacted with local groups who offered the Sacraments only according to the older liturgical books.

Around 2001 my wife and I started a business that sold used, rare and out-of-print Catholic books. Finding old books was a treasure hunt that also exposed us to our vast Catholic literary tradition. We searched for books at auctions, library book sales, estate sales, thrift shops you name it. Sometimes we would buy complete libraries from shuttered seminaries and fading religious orders, once, actually removing hundreds of books from a dumpster.

Carol died in 2002 with no children. Her husband Maurice and her sister preceded her. The contents of her estate was being administered by her cousin, who, through a referral from a friend, I got in contact with about coming to see the collection of books to purchase.

After walking up a long lane boarded by rows of huge maple trees, I arrived at the house on Umpawaug Hill. Inside I found the interior of the uninhabited house dominated by a large central stone hearth, and the room was dotted with colonial style furniture appropriate to the style. Across from the fireplace hung a large portrait of St. Thomas More in a gilded frame. Thomas' countenance seemed to stand guard over the whole place. The floorboards squeaked underfoot and the air had the smell of old-growth hardwood and books. Lots of books.

In the central living areas of the 2,000 square foot house Carol had every bare wall turned into custom built-in bookshelves that reached floor to ceiling. And all of them were filled. Likewise the upstairs rooms were full of her books and the attic contained books that had belonged to her mother and sister. The kitchen, too, was full of books and the loft of the barn held the overflow. Truly an incredible collection, Carol kept a library of all manner of titles by Catholic thinkers, history, poetry, theology, art.

I set to filling cardboard boxes with the books to bring them home to catalog and sell them to our customers online. Many of the books had laid untouched for a long time and were covered in a thick layer of dust on the top edge. Her prayer books and Divine Office were well thumbed as were other books probably used for reference. Many volumes, like a well worn English translation of the Summa Theologica, contained her underlines and handwritten notes in pencil in the margins. Sometimes I would find letters, postcards and prayer cards holding pages within the volumes. These I always saved and set aside.

After a few days' work and a few Uhaul trips back and forth the books were cleared out and the family was happy to see it so. We sent these books to many happy homes around the globe over the next few years.

Years later I saw that Arouca Press was publishing the complete works of Carol Robinson. I was so happy to see her work continue to be recognised. She wrote in that era where they were whitewashing the paintings on the walls of her parish and so many things in the Church and society seemed to be going off the rails. Carol was one of many unsung faithful during those days who, maybe like Medieval monks in cell and cloister who copied and preserved great works—they preserved and used books and wrote and prayed in defense of the true faith of Christ and for the good of the Church.

Today, at Carol's parish in Georgetown, the ancient Mass has returned. Statues have been brought down from the rafters and reinstalled, the high altar has been returned to its place of honor, and the sacred tones of Gregorian Chant and sacred Polyphony again ring out. The pews are once again full and overflowing. Deo Gratias.

Rodger Phillips

1958

1

Naturally Good
APRIL 20, 1958

H AVE YOU EVER RUN INTO A PERSON WHO seemed to be "naturally good"?

There are such people, and they are a challenge to Christians. For instance, they may never offend against charity. Not a word of detraction passes their lips, not an unkind thought seems to darken their minds. They appear honest, upright, self-sacrificing, faithful, and happy. They are all this without the sacraments, without concern about God; indeed without feeling the need of God.

Stumbling, imperfect Christians who live around such a paragon of effortless virtue can't help asking themselves: "How can he be so good without Christ's help"? They start searching for hidden faults, and then are ashamed. Or they take comfort in thinking that for all his natural goodness he will not get to Heaven without supernatural grace, and are ashamed again. For the Christians are not really jealous, and they wish the naturally good person no ill. What they are groping for is the strengthening of their own faith. Christ came to redeem us, and here is somebody who apparently needs no redemption. Christ brought the inestimable gift of grace, which now they are tempted to esteem less.

Surely in such cases the thing to do is to refer the mystery to God and rejoice quite simply in our neighbor's goodness. Maybe these people are not as good as they seem. Maybe trials await them which will bring them to the Faith.

Maybe they are blessed with extraordinary temperamental aids. Never mind. We know that even sinners can do some naturally good things. We know that everyone needs grace to be saved, and that some need more grace than others just to stay out of jail. Let our probing stop there.

However, there is a parallel situation in the world today, and this does deserve some probing because we are not familiar with the underlying principles. It is the challenge of natural goodness, or natural effort, succeeding without the help of Christianity and even succeeding in areas where Christianity seems to have failed.

For instance, there is the increasing dependence on psychiatry to straighten out what used to be considered spiritual or moral problems, and to show people how to live well.

There is the promise of organized medical research to wipe out afflictions where Christianity previously could only comfort the victims.

There is the case of Sweden and certain other countries, where many social injustices have been abolished both without bloodshed and without direct or indirect Christian participation.

Above all there are the triumphs of modern technology and science, which have led to the current simultaneous reorganization of the earth and exploration of space. Christian apologists used to say that our post-Christian world was living on the intellectual capital of the Christian Middle Ages, and maybe this is true but it no longer seems half so convincing. Certainly many great scientists don't think so. They contend that religion was the awe men felt in face of the mysteries of the universe which they themselves are now probing; that faith has now given way to knowledge, but scientific knowledge, not the sight of God.

One could multiply instances, but these suffice for the moment to reveal the threat they present to our faith. It is not that men are denouncing the Church but that they, like a "naturally good" neighbor, unintentionally disparage Christianity by accomplishing so much without its aid. Let us honestly admit as much. Then let us consider what we can do about it.

It is not becoming of us to stand on the side lines looking for flaws and failures: nor to retire into some fortress of our own making, there to prophesy doom for the modern world. And we would be ashamed if we did.

We are trying to guard our faith, but these are not ways to guard it.

It is much better to strengthen our faith with understanding, to see what God intends for this world of ours, to determine the relevance of Christianity to temporal affairs.

That is what this column means to investigate. It will not pretend to lift the veil of mystery which shrouds God's providential workings in the world just as it does the workings of grace in each of us. Instead it will present relevant dogmatic truths along with what might be called "likely applications."

To borrow a phrase from Saint Thomas, our intention is not to prove anything to unbelievers but to instruct and console the faithful.

2

The Salt of the Earth
APRIL 27, 1958

(Original Editor's Note: *Last week we introduced the first of a series of columns by a young woman who is known to the readers of* Integrity *as Carol Jackson and to readers of her books as Peter Michaels. But Carol Jackson is really Mrs. Maurie Robinson and happy about it so from now on we'll identify her that way. This column which we believe to be a most important contribution to Catholic lay thinking is written by Carol Robinson.*)

S O FAR AS A WAY OF LIFE IS CONCERNED, there is a greater difference between us and our grandparents than between our grandparents and, say, the ancient Romans. Upheavals and changes in society occur every so often, but the ones we are now living through are swifter and more drastic than any in the past. This very fact is sufficient to account for many of our problems.

It is not the change in itself which disturbs Christians, but the fact that the new world seems to be forming without Christ. Science is revolutionizing our control over matter, socialism is reorganizing society, the U. N. is adjudicating between political bodies and psychiatry is handling personal problems. Soon these agencies will have established the framework of the future. If Christianity is excluded now, how will it get so much as a foot in the door later?

So we see Christians making frantic efforts to get in on the planning before it is too late. Some are sending telegrams to Congress urging legislators not to lessen our overseas appropriations. Some want to turn out Oppenheimers or Einsteins in Catholic schools. Some are going as lay missionaries to Africa or Latin America. Some are wringing their hands or pumping up emotion or running around in circles. But most of us are doing nothing, because we don't know what to do.

In order to judge the merits of efforts which are being made and to begin making some of our own, we must understand how Christianity is related to the world.

The key is found in Christ's statement: YOU ARE THE SALT OF THE EARTH.

Notice that Christ said we are the salt of the earth, not that we should go be the salt of the earth. What He told us to go do was missionary and apostolic work (go teach all nations and baptize them). He must have meant to insofar as we were really Christian we couldn't help being the salt of the earth.

So first of all we must not feel we are letting Christ down if we are not as bright or rich or important as unbelievers. Some of us are, and some of us aren't. Christ has also described us as leaven, which means we act as yeast wherever we are, but where we are and what we are is normally determined by nature, circumstance and talent, which God uses but does not normally override.

Now since we are salt we must examine the nature and role of salt. Salt is not another ingredient, it is seasoning. It loses itself in the dish, and in so doing makes the dish taste better (not taste it). Salt is a preservative too, but chiefly it makes food palatable.

So Christ has told us that our presence makes temporal life palatable (and preserves it from decay).

It follows that without Christianity life on this earth tends to be tasteless. We learn this from experience, but it is hard to demonstrate. For instance, last week we mentioned Sweden, a model secular welfare state. The complaint in

Sweden is that life is dull. And this is easy to understand, since temporal and even material considerations have been made the be-all and end-all. The same result can be expected from the "American Way of Life." Both are like life without love; adequate, even luxurious, but hardly worth living.

Or again, it is a great achievement of sorts to journey to the moon, which is surely a barren place when you get there. Certain dissatisfied people travel everywhere in search of happiness never to find it because they bring themselves along. If they could first make peace with their own souls, afterwards they could travel or not, as fitted a now purposeful life. Such travel, if any, would be enriching. So it is with the exploration of space. It does not contain its own purpose but must borrow its meaning from higher ends.

These off-hand examples indicate in a general way that the new secular order promises to be drab. Man does not live by bread alone. Bread is a shining goal only to the starving.

We must hasten here to note the one necessary condition of our piquancy. We do not have the power to season the world because we occupy important posts (some of us do, and some of us don't), but, as Christ says, on condition that we do not lose our savor. The one thing which makes us different from other men is that we share God's life by supernatural grace. This grace is our savor. It elevates and transforms us through our minds and our wills, and so through our acts. Christ is telling us that these changed acts, which we think of as means to our own salvation, have inevitable and beneficent repercussions on the affairs of this world.

He also said that if we lose our savor we are fit only to be trod upon by men. We do not revert to the neutral position of those who never had savor, but to the disgrace of those who have failed their mission.

We are the salt of the earth whether we consciously intend it or not. Our solicitude must chiefly turn toward being properly salted.

3

The Conspicuous
Absence
MAY 4, 1958

F ATHER DIVINE, THE NEGRO PREACHER WHO
claims to be God, has some curious expressions. Once
he promised his followers that he would surely attend
a certain function either in his personal presence or in
his personal absence.

His personal absence — a wonderful expression.

It's a pity people so seldom look for the absence of
God in human affairs. There are psychiatric case histories which go on for hundreds of pages, prying into the
sex secrets of grandparents and probing the most trifling
incidents and most casual dreams for clues to mental
breakdown, without ever bothering to inquire if the patient
has been baptized. There are libraries of books on juvenile
delinquency which see everything except the soul and its
relation to God.

It's as though people who knew nothing about cooking
were studying the unpalatability of a stew. Upon analysis
they would discover the chief ingredients, make a scientific study of the most felicitous proportion of carrots
to meat, experiment with the quantity of water and the
degree of heat, even weigh the relative merits of different
cooking utensils.

But they would not (on our hypothesis) see the absence
of salt; nor would they suspect from knowing salt in

isolation, the power it has to perfect a well-proportioned stew, or to render mediocre mixtures reasonably agreeable. By contrast a cook would spot the absence of salt right away.

Now the eyes of faith have a certain power to see the absence of grace. It's not that we Christians can go around knowing who is in a state of grace (we can't even be positive we are). But we know the general necessity of grace, and in certain cases we know its specific availability, from which we can deduce its absence.

As a case in point, we know that the Sacrament of Matrimony carries with it God's promise of grace as needed to preserve the marital union.

What does this enable us to see about marriage that is hidden from the eyes of non-believers? Well, we can see all that they see, PLUS, in certain cases, the conspicuous absence of a factor which would have made a decisive difference.

Curiously enough, the presence of the special matrimonial grace is less marked than its absence, because after all even non-sacramental marriage is holy and harmonious with nature. Marriages should normally endure, and they have abundant help from God in a general way apart from this added help which we are considering. Many of them do succeed on this basis. Even a stable sacramental marriage may or may not depend for its stability on this special supernatural help.

It is with marriages which fail that we are to look for the special absence. Grace may be doubly absent for not having been even promised, as is the case with non-sacramental but valid unions. Or grace may be absent because rejected by husband and/or wife, though proffered by God.

Everyone knows how many clear and sufficient reasons for failure are usually present: money troubles, in-law troubles, temperamental incompatibilities, housing difficulties, immaturity of character, and faults, faults, faults.

Factors such as these, which are frequently cited as causes of divorce, are really contributory rather than decisive causes, for many a marriage has stood its ground in the precise circumstances in which another has given way. The truth is that marriages collapse when things get awful beyond the point of endurance.

We may therefore presume that the grace which God specifically promises works both to prevent or modify the awfulness (especially the awfulness which is personal rather than circumstantial) and to fortify the endurance of the spouses.

Let us go back for a moment to those who see not quite everything. They include most of the people who are doing marriage counseling in one capacity or another. Who can blame them for overconfidence when there is such a rich field for improvement? So they try everything from budgets to psychoanalysis, and these failing the partners try divorce and remarriage.

Sometimes the union is propped up enough to continue somehow on its own, and sometimes the second effort at marriage seems more suitable from a natural point of view (disregarding the question of its validity for the moment). But generally the success of these purely human efforts is not dazzling.

"See here," we might say, "it is true that this marriage is on the rocks because he and she, being far from perfect, and provoked by such-and-such external circumstances, daily exaggerate each other's faults. Still, if they had, and used, special graces which Christian marriage makes available, they could have made a go of it."

And the answer would be: "How do you know"?

And we would say: "Because God is so good that He has promised help, which we know about through faith . . ."

But then, they have no faith, so they can't see.

However, we can know, and we can be consoled by the fact that, where God is allowed to do so, He is holding the very fabric of society together.

What all Christians know by faith, many a Christian husband and wife knows by experience; indemonstrable to others, confused even to them, but deeply a matter of gratitude:

"I would have been a nag..."

"I could have been unfaithful..."

"We might have quarrelled as much as they..."

"Into this same divorce court, but for the grace of God..."

4

Utopia
MAY 18, 1958

SOMEONE OUGHT TO ASK THE HOLY FATHER what kind of world it is he's aiming at, so we Catholics can get working on it.

After all, Karl Marx was very specific about his coming world order, the socialists have plans for theirs down to the least detail, and even the average American can give a general picture of our national ideal.

Isn't it curious then that in all the volumes of modern papal directives on the social order, there just is no such great overall plan for the temporal order? The Popes can't even decide whether they really favor monarchy or democracy, side with this nation or that.

Pius XII is an interesting case in point. He's very specific about what he's against—everything from socialism to euthanasia. He's wonderfully encouraging in a general way to all groups, from bus drivers to scientists and physicians. He praises communications techniques, space exploration, medical research and sundry economic experiments. He's a regular gold mine of guidelines and cautionary remarks. But no plan.

We know where Marxists stand. They are going to wipe out all class distinctions, private property, and, eventually, the state. Only workers will remain, spontaneously unselfish and without need of government, because the causes (economic) of injustice have been eliminated.

We also know about the socialist picture. It centers around the absolute righteousness of the welfare state, which will be all powerful and non-discriminatory in its total solicitude.

And we Americans know that Utopia will be first of all democratic. Not just democratic politically, but also socially. There will be no distinction of race, color or creed. Everyone will be on approximately the same economic level, which will be rich. Not rich in the old way of big estates, servants and capital assets, but in the new way of high wages immediately spent on dream homes and pleasure, while sundry social measures provide protection against possible rainy weather. Our ideal will be achieved (indeed, almost is) more by industrial science and daring than by political change or revolution. The natural friendliness and generosity of the American character will provide the unction.

But why doesn't the Pope have a plan?

He does.

It's God's plan that the Pope has, and indeed is steward of.

Now if God has a plan, that's it. Either we fit in with it, or we fail. There are no alternative schemes that will work. If God intends us to be perfect as He is perfect, we cannot modestly aim at the perfection of the higher animals or of machines. If it is His design that this world be a temporary abode during our period of trial, we cannot humbly say it is lovely enough for us here, we'll dig in comfortably and never mind about Heaven.

There are a lot of things wrong with the schemes mentioned above, but their main fault, which is the source of all their errors, is their implicit denial or disregard of God's scheme. They are human fabrications, non-possible alternatives to God's plan.

The Marxists' great goal is perfect justice, or rather revenge. The poor are going to be exalted and inherit the earth. In God's plan, revenge and perfect justice are His prerogatives.

The socialists are so anxious to have the material side of life neat and orderly that they stifle and bind man's freedom of spirit. God is not that anxious about housekeeping.

As for the Americans (at least the Americans of the illustrated magazines) they are like thoughtless children, so busy having *fun* almost giving the lie to the description of our earthly sojourn as a valley of tears.

God's plan is not for equality, or for guaranteed material well being, or for a surfeit of the good things of this earth.

It is for men to become almost divine and to participate in God's own life for all eternity.

It is not Utopia that God is planning for us, because Utopias have to be realized in this world. Neither is it Paradise, for the innocence proper to that state has passed.

It is Heaven.

As the Holy Father is, so to say, caretaker of the means of getting to Heaven, it is understandable that he won't dream up a blueprint for some ersatz heaven-on-earth.

That does not mean he is not interested in this world. He's very interested. The only thing is that we have to go to him with the right question, which runs something like this:

"What temporal conditions tend to help, and what to hinder, men's salvation?"

5

The Secret Ingredient (Not Money)

MAY 25, 1958

A TV COMMERCIAL ASSURES US THAT THE secret ingredient in a certain coffee is money. Translated, this means it tastes better because it costs more.

Note the faulty logic. The coffee in question tastes better, if it does, because of the bean or the blend. It may be that better tasting beans or blends are in fact more expensive than less good ones, but this is not axiomatic, and has not been proved.

The same specious reasoning runs through contemporary society, with money always the secret ingredient which makes for success or superiority. What is most secretive about money is how it can cure so many alien diseases. One can see it as the precise remedy for bankruptcy, but it is hard to see how it is the paramount factor in a cure for cancer (sure, research laboratories cost money, but genius cannot be bought), in producing more and better nurses (they were more numerous and devoted when they were paid much less, but again not *because* they were paid less), and above all in improving education (which has a closer relationship to truth than to bricks).

The fact that money is usually *necessary* doesn't justify its present exaltation as an elixir. What has happened is that men have acquired a kind of mystical faith in the power of money to transcend itself. This is because they have lost vital contact with the real secret ingredient of a successful world.

When the Holy Father says that Christ is the key to world peace, our secular world thinks he is talking pious and romantic double-talk, relating two unrelated terms. So men turn back with relief to Reason.

Observing increasing *moral* disorder (juvenile delinquency et al) they hasten to apply an *intellectual* remedy (more, and more widespread education), which in turn they hope to achieve by *monetary* means (bigger appropriations).

It's like going down a scale, trying to remedy the higher by the lower. But always ending up at money, no matter what the problem.

"You have to go the other direction to find the secret ingredient, Mr. Reason."

"What direction?"

"Like the Pope said: up."

"Why?"

"Well, if your logic were better you would at least have kept your remedies on par with your diseases — spiritual cures for moral diseases, etc., but as long as you are looking for a universal remedy, you may as well know there is one."

"What is it?"

"You might say it is a sort of infusion of the Divine. It's higher than the human order. We call it *grace*."

"No thanks, I don't need any outside help. I'm not trying to get to Heaven and play harps, I'm just trying to make this present world an orderly, prosperous, well run place. I've got all the tools I need. That logical error, there, it was just a slip."

"Well, good luck! By the way, how does it happen, since you have been trying for so long, that you haven't succeeded?"

"You don't understand. It's taken all of history so far for us humans to come of age, to perfect our own power."

"You mean the Greeks and the Romans weren't very bright? Or maybe that we who are alive now dazzle all past ages by our virtue?"

"No, of course I don't mean that. I'm talking about science and technology, our control over nature, that sort of thing."

"Oh, you mean it's taken all this time to get control over matter. I thought you were talking about perfecting humanity. Aren't we getting back to something like money as the universal cure-all"?

"All right, all right, skip it. Let's see what you have to offer. Can you name me one single human thing that men *can't* do without that grace of yours?"

"No."

"Can't name a single one, huh?"

"No. I wouldn't put any one human virtue or accomplishment outside the range of human effort."

"So you agree with me?"

"On the contrary. To get back to what I said before; if you can, why don't you? If all human things are humanly possible, why is it that men have not yet succeeded in producing the perfect human being, or the perfect world, or even a moderate facsimile of either? Seems like if they can do any particular one, they should be able to do it all."

"Yeah. Well, I dunno. What's *your* explanation?"

"I think it's because men are suffering from a congenital disease which might be described as *the general and diffused inability to live up to the human standard*. So naturally the world suffers a parallel weakness."

"Never heard of this disease."

"We usually call it original sin."

"Oh, that! Don't believe in it."

"Well, as I said before, good luck with our efforts. And if you ever come around to *our* diagnosis, remember that it's grace, for that extra push."

6
Chacun À Son Gout
JUNE 1, 1958

I T IS SAID THAT THERE IS NO ACCOUNTING FOR
tastes.

There ought also to be no meddling with tastes.

Test No. 1 of a good world is this: *It respects the variety God put in the human race.*

Tastes differ because men differ, and men differ primarily because of the material element in their constitutions. Almost all differences in taste, whether they follow broad racial or temperamental patterns, or are peculiar to the individual, are traceable to our different sorts of bodies. This is true even where the predilections seem to be intellectual or spiritual.

One man's meat is another man's poison, because the two men have differently constituted or habituated stomachs.

Some like it hot and some like it cold, fortunately, or everyone would crowd into Miami or Copenhagen. It is because there are those of us who are hot blooded and those of us who are cold blooded; the swimmers and the skiers.

It's beyond them what he sees in her, but he does see something in her which vibrates with something in him and helps strengthen them both against the lure of those more lavishly adorned by nature.

Some gentlemen prefer blonds, but others prefer brunettes. Some go for slant eyes and yellow skins; some for the lithe and some for the hefty. There is no Miss Universe, only Mrs. Smith and Mrs. Paleteri.

Jack Sprat could eat no fat and his wife could eat no lean, which made for a compatible marriage. Sometimes opposites attract and complement each other. Sometimes, or in other respects, it is like which draws like.

There are houses which are just plain ugly (transgressing the laws of visual harmony) and so have a certain basic similitude. But of pleasing houses (and colors and saints and flowers and amusements and professions) there is a luxurious variety, and even an orderly variety.

Though Spanish architecture is suited in a general way to arid regions and tropical vegetation, its patios and casement windows can be endlessly rearranged. Spring flowers in their profusion are different in type from autumn flowers in their profusion.

If you think about it you will realize that only the Divine can be all things to all people without multiplying itself or regimenting men. As this world is in the natural order, it has to accommodate itself to human differences by a kind of kaleidoscopic process, forming and reforming patterns of life throughout the duration of history and reaches off space.

Let us put contemporary society to Test No. 1 of a good world. Does it respect, and accommodate itself, to human diversity?

A mere glance through the picture window of our rubberstamp, split-level house will reveal that the world is much sicker than we thought:

Violating this law, Hitler arbitrarily gave preferential treatment to those of Nordic blood.

Violating this law, Marxists want everyone to be put in the same proletarian straitjacket.

Violating this law, the victorious nations of the last war imposed a democratic form of government on Japan and sundry other peoples, some very primitive, who lacked taste, desire, tradition, or competence for self-government. (Note that this despotism, though well intentioned, was far more drastic and far reaching than colonialism, for it transformed overnight the basic patterns of life.)

Violating this law, some of us deny the privileges of full citizenship to others for reasons of skin pigmentation alone. Violating this law, certain others among us try to force friendships and other close associations among those of disparate intelligences and cultures and among their children, in the name of racial equality.

Violating this law, socialist and welfare states throughout the world increasingly regiment even the personal lives of their citizens, by decreeing how many patients a doctor may have, how many cubic feet of housing space every foster child requires, and how many eggs a family can eat each week.

Violating this law, the American Way of Life, with its photogenic meaninglessness and its shiny, unpaid for machines, is being forced upon us by the relentless velvet gloved pressure of the hucksters.

Violating this law, the development of technology (because it was aimed primarily at profit) concomitantly reduced the masses of western men to irresponsible, interchangeable machine parts, leaving them bewildered, diminished, and prey to exploitation in every direction.

We tried to establish last week that the test of a good world is that it helps rather than hinders men's salvation. How does this first test relate to the matter of our redemption?

God intended that men should be at ease in this world, and that each man should have an area in which he could grow and expand by molding it to his taste. If this is achieved, it will not in itself save us (the Church is the instrument for that) but it will offer no friction.

If the area of personal choice in morally indifferent matters is violated or seriously curtailed, men are not at ease and they cannot develop. An unfitting job is like an incompatible wife; a daily and distracting cross, with recurrent temptations to quit. Womb-to-tomb governmental solicitude is like a one room apartment in which you can't repaint the walls without special permission from the landlord. What is a man to do in such a confined place? Drown his frustrations in TV or baseball? Or maybe alcohol?

There is no need to press the point. It is obvious that insofar as the world declines to respect the variety God put in the human race, it puts special obstacles in the way of men's salvation.

Therefore the Church will never sanction such a world.

Therefore Christians ought in charity to work to make it otherwise.

This is not easy, nor are the means of doing so obvious. But the first step is to know it must be worked out.

7

Water is Thicker Than Blood

JUNE 8, 1958

> Humpty Dumpty sat on a wall
> Humpty Dumpty had a great fall
> All the armed forces and all the U. N.
> Couldn't put Humpty together again.

TRADITIONAL CHILDREN'S RHYMES OFTEN bear Christian interpretation. Humpty Dumpty, for instance, may be considered the nursery version of the Fall of Man. He is Everyman, whose internal warfare yields to no human tranquilizer. He is our fragmented world, which cannot find an adhesive strong enough to unify it.

The most encouraging thing that can be said about our fragmented Humpty Dumpty world is that it wants to be made whole. The problem is, how?

Let's examine some of the proposed sticking plasters.

First of all there are those optimists who think Humpty's fall was a pure accident with no lasting consequences. The pieces will go right together again if we just gather them up and put them back on top of the wall.

We are all human beings. Humanity itself is a sufficient bond. There is no intrinsic reason for dog to fight dog, for cats to quarrel with other cats or for men not to get along with other men. They just need to get to know each other better or to be educated or properly trained.

The trouble with this theory is that it runs clean contrary to the facts. Dogs and cats do fight with one another, nations war with nations, and fratricide is not unknown. Since all this has been going on from the dawn of recorded history, it would seem to weigh heavily against the notion that a common species provides sufficient basis for harmony.

In our day men have a new angle for this theory. They say that, taken all together, we men are not just an aggregate, but we are God. This is simply what God is: the whole of creation. Everything has at least a spark of the divine and men reflect that in flames of varying sizes and degrees. This divinity in which we all share develops over a period of time, and at the fulfilment of its evolutionary growth, men will be somehow transfigured by the maturation of their natural divinity. Then global harmony will prevail.

Whenever you hear men speak of Humanity with a capital "H" and in awed tones, you can be pretty sure they are worshipping their collective selves.

The trouble with this theory is that it is not true. It mistakes God's presence in the world by immensity (which is the power by which He holds creation in existence) with God's own nature and internal life. It is the current version of the classical error of Pantheism.

So much for the idea of an internal harmony. There is another set of theories which counts on some sort of felicitous external arrangement for the world's adhesive.

The cruder sort of these theories counts on naked force. It holds that peace and order in the world or in a particular country are simply to be found in the achievement of one all-powerful dictator making efficient use of strength and restraint. Hitler, Trujillo,* and a multitude of other examples both ancient and modern spring to mind.

---

* Rafael Leónidas Trujillo Molina (October 24, 1891–May 30, 1961), dictator of the Dominican Republic who ruled from 1930 until 1961 when he was assassinated.

Though tyranny is terrible while it lasts, it never seems to last very long. On the whole it is less dangerous to humanity than certain intellectual theories.

These intellectual theories look for the external adhesive in organization. Force may be necessary in the reorganization process (this is what the Marxists hold, for instance) but once the world has been rearranged according to "rational" norms, harmony will prevail because a natural equilibrium will have been achieved.

Thus the elimination of private property will end contests for material possessions. The leveling of classes will wipe out the hatred previously caused by inequality. The exaltation of the workers will end injustice and revolution forever. Mass production will satisfy all needs and quell all desires.

Guaranteed security will give peace of mind. One central world political organization will stop national friction. If any quarrelling remains because of human nastiness, this will disappear with the remaking of human nature by eugenics and psychiatry.

These major "norms" of rationality are shared in varying degrees by all secularists, and they represent what men in our day come to believe when they set themselves in God's place.

The only real opposition comes from Christians who try to search out and respect the way God has ordered the world. Here is what they find:

That there really is a built in basis for harmony in the human race, because we are all blood relations.

That there is considerable natural harmony to be found in the world, even today, where the blood relationship is close, as in families and ethnic groups.

That the failure of men to complete and sustain this natural harmony stems from a congenital weakness — original sin.

That disharmony is aggravated by external disorders which result from our accumulated sins, not because of classes or property or inequality as such.

That in God's plan men are to be reunited by water, the water of Baptism. They are no longer to be just fellow members of the human family distantly related by blood. They are now to be brothers of Christ and so of each other, branches of one vine, living by one same divine life. The most naturally diverse among them are to be brought closer to each other in charity, than to their own close blood relations in a human way.

That this new higher community of men transcends without destroying the partial truths in the false theories. It is built on the natural unity of blood (Christ is the new Adam). It binds men by a love so powerful that it can tranquilize all human discord. With it men can bring about external conditions which support and reinforce harmony.

That is why the Holy Father says that Christ is the key to world peace.

8

A Healthy World
JUNE 15, 1958

A HEALTHY WORLD IS LIKE A HEALTHY STOM-
ach—it functions without calling attention to itself.
As a matter of fact, the world is a kind of house
for the human race, just as the body is a kind of house
for the soul.

So when we ask, "What is a good world?," we can think
in terms of "What is a good body?"

Then we can answer right away that for one thing it
is healthy.

Our practical test of bodily health is that we feel no pain
or weakness. The same test applies to emotional and mental
health. The non-neurotic person feels what the situation
calls for, and he is not overpowered by unnatural joy or
some murky resentment or sorrow which arises from his
own unbalanced constitution. He can learn and analyze
objectively without going through an agony of introspection,
or twisting facts to his own distorted viewpoint.

A healthy person need not have bulging biceps, or an
IQ of 160. He simply has a normally functioning physical
and mental apparatus, which serves him well without distracting him from his proper pursuits, and which does not
demand more than routine care.

A healthy world is one in which there is good order, justice, stable government, harmonious economic operations
and cooperative amity among classes and peoples. It is a
world which provides in an orderly way for the disciplining

of men's minds in the truth, and the development of men's gifts for the common and individual good.

In such a world a man may grow and develop, pursue his calling, raise a family and adore God, without being prevented or diverted by external catastrophe and disorder.

But how will a man fare in a diseased world? What if there is no stable government in his country, only a succession of usurping dictators? What if wars and invasions occur every generation?

What if the periods between wars are marked by cold wars or armed truces which paralyze normal pursuits? What if error is rife in the schools and universities? What if marriage and morals and home life are undermined by legal license?

What if business and workmen's associations are the prey of gangsters? What if unjust economic conditions cause the rich to grow richer to the point of wallowing in luxury, and the poor to sink to destitution? What if communities are torn apart and families are uprooted?

What if even legitimate governments are weighted down with bureaucracies and so corrupted by special interests that they act only to bind the populace in the fetters of legal minutiae? What if riots, hunger strikes and subversive activities must constantly be quelled?

Obviously, to live in such a world without despairing, a man will need to be a hero. That is why the Church regards a sick world, or a sick body, as a hindrance to salvation. And that is why she encourages good doctors of all sorts.

One can read the social encyclicals of the Popes as though they were textbooks of social medicine. There one will find the disease of society diagnosed and analyzed in detail, the principles of sound health clearly enunciated, and remedies suggested. Every doctor (apostle) will have to make prudential applications to his own field, but he has the general guidelines.

He also has the assurance that his is a work of charity, as is the work of a medical doctor. Neither directly teaches men to love God, but both are removing impediments to the effective love of God.

It is interesting to note that each kind of doctor's healing activity works to eliminate the need for the doctor. A healed wound is soon forgotten, a job soothes the pain of unemployment. Patients who have recovered lose interest in the doctor as well as in their ailments, and turn to the normal pursuits of life. Ill health hurts, but health doesn't feel at all.

Thus it is that social justice and physical health are not ultimate goals of life, but just functioning norms of the social and physical bodies. This does not make them unimportant. Nor is there any chance that the pursuit of these norms will become unnecessary. The poor and the sick will always be with us.

What we should learn from this analogy is that the social apostle, even as the medical doctor, should bow out at the precise moment when he has eliminated the need for his services. Let him turn to another illness or another patient.

Medical doctors know better than social doctors how to judge this point. Many a social worker and lay apostle makes the mistake of thinking that if health is good, more health is both better and possible. But health is a norm and does not admit of degrees on the way to some final perfection.

When the body functions well, one should forget it, not go on to become a physical culture crank or food faddist.

If workmen must be organized for self protection in the face of money power, let them be so organized. But if they are carried away by their newfound strength and use it to get disproportionately rich at the expense of the common good, if they hold society up for ransom whenever it please them, then trade unionism ceases to be a crusade (an act of charity) and becomes in its turn the cause of other diseases (presumption, sloth, disregard of the common good, gangsterism, avarice) which hinder salvation in their turn, and need a quite different and more drastic remedy.

Lay apostolic groups have sometimes been accused (especially in France) of falling inadvertently into the Communist camp in their fight for social justice. This can happen when such groups pursue the norm of social well being beyond reasonable limits. One day their work is seen to have lost its link with God's work of redemption, and they find themselves building an earthly paradise with the materialists.

9

The Devil and Eve's Many Faces
JUNE 22, 1958

I DON'T KNOW THAT EVELYN LANCASTER, THE present incumbent of a body originally belonging to Eve White, is possessed by the devil or is a possessing devil. However, I think the possibility exists.

In any case, the doctors concerned with this famous instance of "multiple personality" have added confusion to mystery by their dogmatic secularism. Let us try to reorient the facts in their light of certain philosophical and theological truths.

The case of Eve's several faces has been widely publicized in articles, books and a movie. At first Eve had three faces. Now (*Life* magazine, May 19th) she has a fourth face, and that is not too firm. An autobiography of this fourth face, who calls herself Evelyn Lancaster, was published 13 days after the *Life* article, but was written earlier. It was overly confidently entitled, "The Final Face of Eve." The word "face," of course, is a euphemism for the different something-or-other who inhabit and use the same human body.

There have been other cases of so-called "multiple personality." The best known is that of Dr. Jekyll and Mr. Hyde, which happens to be fictitious but does illustrate the sort of phenomenon encountered. One and the same body appears to be occupied alternately or successively by distinctly different and often contrasting people.

The impression that there are *several* persons involved is always strongly attested. Yet human nature consists of the union of one soul with one particular body. Are we to suppose that rarely and freakishly there can be multiple souls united to one body? This is what the doctors seem willing to admit on the basis of the evidence.

Or are we to hold firmly to our concept of human nature in the face of seemingly contradictory evidence? Here is where the Faith helps us, even in the natural order. The "one soul to one body" concept is philosophical, not scientific. A philosopher can reason to its necessary truth. But as not all men have that much intellectual power, the truth can also be certainly held because of its intrinsic connection with various revealed truths held on the Church's authority.

Now the whole investigation of Eve's case rested on shifting sands because there was no firmly held truth about human nature. Otherwise, the reasoning might have proceeded as follows:

Disregarding the possibility of trickery, two alternative explanations offer themselves: either we have here a continuity of personality with freakish changes, or there are several persons involved, only one of whom is human.

The first alternative is contrary to evidence and testimony all the way down the line. Still it cannot be discarded absolutely unless the second alternative is established as the true explanation.

The second alternative is diabolical possession. As the apparently well meaning doctors seem never even to have entertained this hypothesis, their data will only accidently be pertinent. Even so they have provided much supportive evidence.

It is possible for the devil, or several devils, to possess a human body. There are many cases of such happenings throughout history, including the well known incidents recorded in the Gospels.

There are limits to the devil's power in possession. He cannot occupy the soul. He cannot replace the soul with his own spirit. But he can occupy and operate the body, and he has a certain control over the senses and lower faculties.

The person possessed usually blacks out into unconsciousness when the devil takes over. Although the victim's soul remains in the body and sustains its life, he is powerless to act and usually has no knowledge of what is done by the evil spirit during the blackout period. Eve White's experience exactly matches this theoretical description.

When a possessing devil is not exercising control of the body his inactive presence may not manifest itself at all. This may have been the situation which aroused false hopes of a "cure" or a "final face."

Or again the devil may in his inactive presence be the cause of mysterious chronic infirmities — such as the headaches which are a prominent feature of this case.

The devil also has the power to operate directly on the internal mechanism of the senses, even where it is not a full case of possession. He can make people hear voices when no one has spoken, and see sights that are not in front of their eyes. Eve heard voices.

Although there are also other technical points to support hypotheses of possession, let us pass on to the central problem of good and evil.

The devil is evil, and his purposes are evil. He can possess good people against their will, or bad people with their cooperation.

Now Eve's doctors are vaguely Freudian. Like most psychiatrists today, they are not concerned with good and evil in the moral sense, and even less with the love of God, the life of grace and the matter of salvation. They see conduct as "positive" or "negative." Their idea of human perfection is "adjustment." And because they have superimposed this bias of theirs on their investigation of this case, it is difficult to analyze their findings in moral terms.

What does seem certain is that Eve White was possessed unwillingly, if possessed she was, since the first indication is in early childhood. Besides, she was always on the side of virtue. A fundamentalist type Protestant, she was preoccupied with religion and did her duty as she saw it. It was in a moment of despair under heavy strain and great physical weakness that the second face, Eve Black, really came into power. And later it was when Eve White consented to divorce her husband that she "died." Here again it was a kind of despair, under pressure from the doctors and the other faces, combined with an understandable mental confusion about the path of duty. It was weakness rather than badness, but it led to her dispossession. She has not yet reappeared.

If Eve White was good, Eve Black was bad and could easily have been identified as a visiting devil. But the doctors saw Eve White as guilt-ridden and frigid, and Eve Black as a kind incarnated "Id" who had the very qualities of adjustment the first face lacked. They tried to get Eve Black's cooperation (the last thing you should do if it is really a case of possession) and hoped to make a sort of synthesis of the two personalities.

Instead they got, or anyhow there appeared, a third face, Jane, whom they actually groomed to supersede the first two. Here is a classic illustration of the enormous but unconscious presumption of secularists. Instead of respecting God's creation by trying to establish the rightful possessor in Eve's body, they were quite ready and anxious to install the face most pleasing to their prejudices.

With the consideration of the third and fourth faces the contrast between good and evil yields to the phenomenon of personality deterioration. At first Jane was what the doctors considered mature and balanced, the context of their judgment and her actions being completely unrelated to Christianity.

But after a while Jane kind of went to pieces, did all sorts of odd things, and finally tried suicide. The fourth face just managed to get control of the body in time to save its life.

That fourth face is Evelyn, a sort of prettier and more loving Jane. She was considered the final face because she really was adjusted (A key point: she was the only one of the four not sexually frigid) and because she felt free of the interior presences of the others.

...until she stole a sweater from a department store and started having violent headaches.

Evelyn has since recovered her equilibrium and as of the *Life* article is living in happy togetherness in a trailer camp with her (their) second husband and Eve White's (or their) daughter.

Though I can't help but wish her well, I rather doubt that the final chapter has been written to the tale of the multiple faces of Eve.

10

Are All Men Created Equal?

JULY 6, 1958

"WE HOLD THESE TRUTHS TO BE SELF-EVI-dent...that all men are created equal."

The Fourth of July is a good time to re-examine our American ideals on a deeper level. We are so familiar with the Declaration of Independence that few of us have ever given it mature thought.

Is it true that all men are created equal?

If it is, how are we living up to this ideal?

As to the first question, it is true that all men are created equal in some respects. The companion truth is that all men are created unequal, in other respects.

How are all men equal?

All men are equally men. They all belong to the same species.

But that is not saying anything, is it?

On the contrary, it is saying that all men are different from all mere animals. It indicates how men, as men, have to be treated. All of them alike.

What does that mean in practice?

It follows the line of rationality. Because men have free will they must be dealt with justly rather than arbitrarily. Their consent is necessary for important things, such as marriage. Since they have immortal souls they can never be subordinated entirely to another person's end.

Now what about the inequality?

Men are unequal as compared to each other. They are born with unequal and diverse talents and abilities. These are natural inequalities, which exist before any consideration of injustice or circumstance.

Why doesn't the Declaration of Independence mention that all men are born unequal?

Perhaps because the men who signed it thought the fact was too obvious to mention. They certainly thought that it was more important to stress equality at the time. That's why we have a democracy. It's a form of government which stresses equality rather than inequality. It also stresses freedom rather than order, but we aren't concerned with that here.

Is there a form of government, then, which emphasizes inequality?

Yes, aristocracy. It stabilizes society on the basis of differences and inequalities. It works on strong hereditary lines too, on the principle that natural inequalities are usually transmitted from generation to generation.

Is it true that they are?

Yes, by and large, because the root of the inequalities is our physical nature.

If men are both equal and unequal what happens to the truth which isn't stressed in these forms of government?

It isn't necessarily neglected. It's just that governments can't do everything, so they take particular pains to guard one element and trust non-political means to sustain the other. In real life new forms of governments are often reactions against the abuses of the contrasting forms. That was largely the case with our own country. Not only the Founding Fathers, but the waves of immigrants who followed later, were fed up with monarchies and aristocracies which had decayed and forgotten about the equality of men. They wanted a chance to prove their own worth, and that was what America offered them.

Actually, American democracy counted on freedom of opportunity and universal education to reshuffle society.

There were no arbitrary class barriers. The way was wide open for every man to work hard and rise to his own proper level. It was a wonderful dream!

Did it materialize?

Well, it is a little hard to say what we actually wanted it to do.

We didn't want to build up a class system again, and we haven't. But we didn't get stability either. We cannot point to an appreciable number of solid families in the different walks of life. Incidentally "walks of life" is a euphemism for "class." Never mind.

Neither have we built up much of a natural aristocracy. The cream has not risen to the top and developed a tradition of public service.

We have certainly been the Land of Opportunity, especially the opportunity to get rich.

But there is something very serious happening here in America. A perversion of the whole idea of equality is spreading. It is not now a matter of holding that men are born equal, but that they can be made equal, and made equal in the very ways that they are naturally unequal.

For instance, look hard at our educational system. It is now promoting dull students so as not to hurt their feelings. At the same time it penalizes superior students by holding them to a mediocre level.

Or look at what is happening in trade unions and in certain socialistic political measures. There is a leveling of rewards without respect to merit. It is not hard work or ability or long faithful service which counts, but what men can get by the force of their numbers.

This recent trend cannot be cured politically. It will not be remedied by stirring references to a misunderstood and in itself rather ambiguous Declaration of Independence. It rests on perverted ideas and a general breakdown of virtue and discipline.

Only a general and powerful spiritual revival is strong enough medicine.

11

God's Preference
JULY 13, 1958

"I OFTEN ASKED MYSELF WHY GOD HAS PREF-
erences, why all souls do not receive an equal measure
of grace."

You probably recognize this quotation from the early
paragraphs of the autobiography of Saint Thérèse. It makes
an interesting contrast to the bold assertion of the Declaration of Independence that it is self-evident all men are
created equal.

Our present quotation might be said to come from the
Declaration of Dependence. It states that men are unequal
in the most profound way possible, in the measure of God's
gratuitous love for them.

Of course one of these statements was made in the political order, the other in the spiritual and supernatural order.
Still, they should harmonize, because there is really only one
order in the universe, which is the Divine Plan, though there
are different levels of being which must be respected. Furthermore, we humans live only one life, so that things which
are distinct in themselves must be reconciled in our actions.

Can we, as Americans, always puff out our chests in
boastful proclamation that we are good as anyone else,
and then, as Christians, humbly seek the lowest place?
How shall we square the two ideals of conduct? By taking
the back row in church?

Again, is it fitting for an American politician to exaggerate his qualifications for office, to be photographed on

election day confidently casting a ballot in his own favor? Candidates for the papacy and other religious offices are not even allowed to vote for themselves, because they are humbly to consider themselves unworthy of such high office.

To be sure, an ecclesiastical office far exceeds any human competence, but civil government is a hard job too, one which needs grace in its own proportion.

Some sort of reconciliation is in order if we are to have the mind of Christ with respect to the whole of our lives. Let's start by following through Saint Thérèse's explanation of how things work in the order of grace, and then let us see if there is not some relationship in the matter of inequalities between the supernatural order and temporal affairs.

You will recall that God let Saint Thérèse know that souls taken all together are like a flower garden, more beautiful for its variety, even though the variety involves inequality.

Little flowers, among whom the saint places herself, reflect God's goodness as much as imposing ones. As a matter of fact, since God has to stoop lower to reach them, they draw out more of His goodness.

In this way Saint Thérèse shows that it is humility which elicits God's grace, rather than any positive greatness of our own. It is in accordance with this truth that Our Lord told us to seek the lowest place in recognition of our own unworthiness, so that He can invite us to the head of the table. Since God is free, He prefers whom He prefers, but there is a certain correspondence between our humility and our elevation.

Here in our American democracy, things work quite differently. He who pushes himself hardest usually gets to sit at the head of the table. The enterprising man is the one who becomes rich. The job hunter who "sells himself" lands the job. And the product about which there is the most ballyhoo sells like hot cakes!

Now let's face it: this is disorder. It is not the way things ought to be. It is just the sort of disorder to which democracy is liable, since everything from statesmen to soap is submitted to the unconsidered and easily swayed tribunal of public opinion.

What is the antidote for the disorder?

It would be ridiculous at this point to try to inculcate modest and honest self-appraisal in politicians. The candidate who said that he might, with God's help, do the job but he wasn't sure, would never get a chance to try.

Hard work, long hours and conscientiousness have not nearly the earning power of membership in a high pressure union. If the job seeker doesn't have a big opinion of himself, who will? The product which has only merit to recommend it will find no marketing channels.

The social equilibrium is upset because self-seeking, ambitious men have pushed themselves into the high places they don't deserve. The ultimate reason for this is *fallen* human nature. So the fundamental cure is grace. The way grace restores the equilibrium, is by inspiring *other* men to humility, in some sort of echo of Our Lord's restoration of the human balance after Adam's sin.

Of course local remedies are also in order, but there is not much hope in investigating committees or in stirring the masses to vigilance, simply because these are not even trying to restore the balance. It is the work on the equilibrium which must be a background for all our other efforts. Sometimes, as now, it is of paramount importance.

In recent years we have seen a parade of talented young men enter Trappist monasteries. We may, if we like, look upon this movement as the work of grace restoring balance.

Once we grasp the idea of establishing a counterweight for society we will better understand why grace seems to start a movement in the opposite direction from the disorder. So we should look for a love of poverty to counteract the American standard of living, for detachment as the cure of our transformation into consumers, and for those who will serve as a remedy for pride.

Better still, we can start off in the opposite direction ourselves. We can be confident that our humility will call down God's grace.

12

Incentives
JULY 20, 1958

"WHY CAN'T WE HAVE GOLD STARS FOR courage?" an eleven-year-old asked us, after valiantly climbing out on the roof to retrieve his ball. We had previously presented him with an enormous paper star in recognition of the valor he displayed in making his first solo trip from school in New York to our house in Peekskill, using taxis at both ends.

"Why not?" we decided.

So when he and a twelve-year-old friend arrived to spend two weeks, there were two large poster size placards on the living room wall. Progress Charts, we called them. They were designed by a visiting artist who executed the calligraphy in black and red ink on white in one case, on yellow in the other. Naturally, the boys' names were prominently displayed.

Half the charts were given over to Day-by-Day Habit Formation, in such respects as Helpfulness, Courtesy, Promptness, Cleanliness and Eating for Health. In another section were colored designs for the Achievement Badges I was to embroider on the boys' shirts as the requirements for each were fulfilled. These decorations could be gained for such accomplishments as Bicycling, Marksmanship (3 grades), Junior Journalism (we publish a paper around here from time to time), Letter Writing, Hiking, Worthwhile Reading and Studies in Greatness.

In a third section we rewarded certain acts such as

Truthfulness, Good Deeds, and Courage (moral and physical) as and when they were performed.

We had laid in a large supply of stars of various colors and sizes, which were solemnly pasted on the posters every evening, in the presence of the Head of the House.

It all worked like a charm. Not only were daily duties done with dispatch, but the boys looked around for more work when they were through — so as to earn extra stars for good deeds. We were able to explain to now eager ears how it takes moral courage to learn to ride a bike when everyone else around you is an expert, or to be a good loser at croquet.

Best of all, we were able to heap praises, deserved praises, on the boys' heads, instead of nagging them.

You will be thinking our Progress Charts were just a big steal from the Boy Scouts.

It is true that we borrowed some of our ideas from Scouting, but Titus Caesar was a more direct source of inspiration.

Titus was the Roman General who sacked Jerusalem in 70 A. D. The Jewish historian Josephus described the siege in great detail, since he was present with the Roman army as a captive and intermediary.

The attack on the city had to be made over one wall of the Temple, at first by ladder.

Calling for volunteers for the initial, most difficult, attempt, Titus said: "As for the person who first mounts the wall, I should blush for shame if I did not make him to be envied by others, by those rewards I would bestow upon him. If such a one escapes with his life, he shall have the command of others that are now but his equals..."

Later, as the final attack was being prepared, Titus put on his own armor to lead it, but "his friends would not let him go, by reason of the greatness of the danger... They said he would do more by sitting above in the Tower of Antonia, as a dispenser of rewards to those soldiers that signalized themselves in the fight."

Titus complied only, as he said, so that "he might be able to judge of their courageous actions, and that no valiant soldier might lie concealed, and miss of his reward, and no cowardly soldier might go unpunished..."

And so it was done.

Afterwards, when Jerusalem had been destroyed and the Roman armies were about to depart, Titus thanked all his soldiers and made good his promise, saying that "no one who had been willing to take more pains than another should miss of a just retribution for the same; for that he (Titus) had been exceedingly careful about this matter, and that the more, because he had much rather reward the virtues of his fellow soldiers than punish such as offended."

Then Titus read out the names of the specially courageous. He commended them personally, put crowns of gold on their heads, gave each one a higher rank, and plentifully distributed the spoils among them.

It isn't just soldiers and young boys who need incentives; we all do.

The very word "incentive," indicates its dynamic force. It means to impel to action, to encourage, to set on fire.

We humans are like donkeys. We go forward only if there is a stick behind us and a carrot in front.

Tough necessarily, the stick has a very limited power. The fear of going to jail may lessen crime, but it won't make good citizens. Secret police cannot induce patriotism. The fear of losing one's job provokes only a minimum and begrudging servitude. And though the fear of Hell has presumably saved many a soul, alone it has produced no saints but only those miserable and ignoble Christians who go about enjoying as much as they dare, but less than they would like, of the good things of this world.

Incentives are what ignite our potentialities so that we move toward a goal under our own power. A good world is one full of incentives to self-improvement, conscientiousness and virtue. Our impersonal, mechanized, mass, conformist, cynical civilization has mowed down incentives like grass. One day it will realize that the size of the stick must increase as the carrot disappears.

Meanwhile we see here another of those numerous and inestimable benefits Christianity bestows on an ungrateful society. When nobody knows and nobody cares how well or ill a job is done, religion offers the only incentive: God, Who sees us in secret, and will reward us in Heaven.

13

Didja Read in the Paper?
JULY 27, 1958

"DIDJA READ IN THE PAPER WHAT THE ARCH-
bishop of Canterbury said?"

"No, who's he?"

"He's the head of the Anglican Church. That's what they call the Episcopalian Church in England."

"What did he say?"

"He said God may let us destroy ourselves with nuclear bombs."

"How does he know? Did God tell him?"

"Of course not. He's thinking from theology."

"I don't get you."

"It's this way. We know something about God and how He operates. So we take this matter of nuclear weapons, and we ask if there is any good reason why God would not allow us to blow ourselves to bits."

"Are you assuming that we are trying to blow the human race to bits?"

"No, I just observe that we are in danger of doing so. We have bombs powerful enough, and we are sitting on an international tinderbox."

"Maybe I'm dense, but I don't see the point of the Arch-bishop's statement. What was he trying to prove?"

"So far as I can tell from the newspapers, he wasn't try-ing to prove anything. He was just making a theological comment."

"Unprovoked?"

"No. It's in a book about nuclear policy. Some other people writing in the same book are saying that England ought
to appease the Russians to save their own skins. They figure
the Russians are now stronger than the Western powers."

"And that these are the only alternatives?"

"Apparently. And apparently, too, they would choose life
on any terms rather than extinction."

"Where does the Archbishop stand?"

"It's not clear from the newspaper account. He merely
says that race extinction might be in accordance with
God's plans."

"Is it?"

"Oh yes, but not necessarily now. God has told us that
there will be an end of time."

"When?"

"That's God's secret."

"Maybe it will be now because now we have powerful
enough means to destroy the human race — or we think
we have."

"That's the Archbishop of Canterbury's point. And it may
be that God will choose such a moment. But the end of
the world will come when God's redemptive plans have run
their predetermined course. There is no direct correlation
between the completion of the work of redemption (only
God knows how that will be judged) and our scientific
advancement. Nor does God need us to destroy the world.
It can be done by angels."

"You mean it would be purely coincidental if it came
about that way."

"Coincidental in our perspective, but providential as
worked out by God."

"Still...."

"I know what you are going to say. Still, the very fact
that these nuclear weapons exist is in the nature of a
permanent threat to the human race."

"Exactly."

"So the question is a little changed. It is no longer that of whether God will let us destroy ourselves, but of whether He will prevent it."

"And that's a tough one."

"Not only tough, but indemonstrable."

"How so?"

"Well, let's assume first that the time has not yet come in God's plan for the end of the world. It follows that He will prevent our destroying it in the present circumstances. This He could do by miracles. But God does not ordinarily work by miracles. Let us assume then that He will do it by what we shall call preventive grace."

"What is that?"

"It's a sort of restraining grace. It's like not losing your temper where you ordinarily would, because somehow, subtly, God prevented you. Your patience was somehow lengthened or your attention somehow diverted."

"I see. It looks like you did it yourself."

"Yes, usually. And of course if we get through this, God is not likely to get the credit in high quarters."

"Doesn't Our Lady of Fatima come in here someplace?"

"Yes, it would seem as though God has long had the cooperation of those who have done penance for our whole world. How otherwise can we explain the fact that the forces of evil and of war have been restrained this long?"

"And here we all are, just worrying about our own skins!"

"The whole point is that it's not a battle for skins, it's a battle for souls, but with every military and diplomatic move having potentially far reaching spiritual consequences."

"And you really think that God will use this preventive grace for diplomats and heads of states and soldiers?"

"Yes I do, and I think we should earnestly pray that He will."

14

Of Human Dignity
AUGUST 3, 1958

C ATHOLIC ACTION HAS ALWAYS MADE IT A big point that the worker should know his own dignity.

What is his own dignity? What is ours? What is human dignity?

It's *safe* to say that everyone is on the side of dignity. But it is pathetic to see how many false or inadequate ideas about dignity are in circulation. Let's consider some of them.

The word dignity simply means "worth" in Latin.

"He must be worth a half million dollars," we say, measuring a man's dignity by his wealth.

This is a frequent rule of thumb. We do often bestow respect and honor in proportion to a person's riches. It is one of the crudest manifestations of the materialism of our society. There are more subtle refinements.

For instance, the concomitance of dignity and money sometimes works inversely. As the intrinsic dignity of a man's work declines, he is likely to be paid more. This happens to intellectual workers when they subordinate their efforts directly to money rather than to truth or art. That's why editors and writers, who traditionally have been poor, but respected and influential, now often have luxurious offices, handsome typewriters, and Cadillacs. Their magazines and newspapers have become primarily channels for advertising, which means that all copy must subserve mass circulation.

The advertising men themselves illustrate a slight variation on the materialistic pattern of dignity. They bolster their ego with external appearances rather than money in the bank. Hand painted ties, tailored suits of a special cut, chic-in-a-certain-way wives, and the calculated careless paraphernalia of exurbanite living, all stem from Madison Avenue.

The advertising man needs these props to his self-esteem, because he is giving his time and his often considerable talent to some matter, like the color combination on a detergent's box, which is ludicrously unworthy in itself of so much careful consideration, but which may have resounding financial reverberations in our curiously lop-sided society.

The woman who feels positively naked without lipstick, and the man who is proudly conscious of the tail light arrangement on his new car, both are near of kin to the advertising man. In fact most of us, one way or another, rely on the decor of life, often at its most trifling, for our dignity. This indicates a superficiality of character or of way of life, rather than any deep set avarice.

At almost the opposite pole are what might be called the spiritualists, or the would-be angels. They consider anything material, especially anything physical, as in itself an indignity. They miss the point of human dignity because they refuse to accept human nature. The union of body and soul seems to them to be a misfortunate, from which the soul should make every effort to withdraw.

Here are the people who want to separate the marriage bed from marriage. Here are the neurotics who have an abnormal horror of sickness or dirtiness or nakedness. Here, doctrinally, are the Christian Scientists, who pretend the body isn't there.

Actually, on account of the Fall, the body has a powerful influence on our human dignity. Just as a disciplined body protests us from sin, so a clean and modestly clothed body guards our human dignity. That is why decent living quarters can be such a great spiritual help to a family. And that is why the so-called "indignities" of concentration camps can destroy the morale of all but the strongest of us.

Another half truth about human dignity is that we can hold up our heads only so long as we are useful.

Anyone who has been unemployed knows how self-respect suffers from not being needed or wanted by society. Yet it is an error to suppose that human dignity must rest on productiveness. There are weak and handicapped people who are burdens to society all their lives. Are they therefore without human dignity?

Besides, all of us will come to the end of our term of usefulness if we live long enough. Why should old age be asked to justify itself in the one respect in which it will surely sometime fail?

We are youth worshippers as a natural consequence of our being sensate, materialistic and pragmatic. So we are embarrassed by old age. Beauticians try to disguise our many years. Swarms of social workers go on about remunerative hobbies, or post-retirement jobs, as though all would be lost if we didn't work until we dropped, or at least if we didn't have fun until we drew our last breath.

Oddly enough, old age is a time of natural dignity, because it is a period far removed from the storms and ambitions of life. It is a period of wisdom, a time for rest. It is the special time of preparation for death.

Nobody has to embellish old age with a phony dignity. All we have to do is to let old people be old, and to pay them honor.

Now let us come to the worker, who is trying so hard to retrieve his dignity. He, too, is urged to consider his usefulness. He is reminded of the complexity of modern society, of how many men contribute to the production of an automobile or the making of a loaf of bread, of how dependent we all are on the concerted efforts of the masses of workers.

Somehow it never is quite convincing, although the worker himself can't figure out quite why. It is because in our mechanized society no factory worker or farm hand counts for much in himself. He is generally an undifferentiated, replaceable, unskilled part of a non-viable, collective whole which gets things done. As such he does not have human dignity, but a kind of apiarian dignity. His is merely the busyness of the honey bee, as better than the idleness of the drone.

Honesty will serve us here. Let us admit that although human beings ought to have a certain appropriate dignity, they have been robbed of much of it by our disordered society and our false philosophies. For many of us there is simply no hope of regaining a proper human dignity.

This situation is not helped, but worsened, by the well intentioned but ignorant people who go about perverting the very idea of human dignity.

Only Christianity can salvage the situation.

15

How to Make an Omelette
AUGUST 10, 1958

"YOU CAN'T MAKE AN OMELETTE WITH ROTTEN eggs."

So the saying goes. Of course it also means you can't make a good world with bad people. You can, however, make a good world order, or a fairly good one, with defectible people. That's lucky, because defectible is what we are.

Our personal problem is to make a new world order, suited to a new stage of world growth, with eggs which have already begun to smell.

Messers Eisenhower, Khrushchev, Dulles and so on down to the least of those in charge of the common good—these are the cooks. Finding a good new recipe is their headache.

We are the somewhat less than fresh eggs.

Unfortunately human eggs can't be thrown out in favour of newer and fresher ones. But human freshness can be renewed, with the help of grace.

We eggs should be seeing to our own freshness, but you would think from the looks of things that our job was to advise and supervise the cooks.

It is in accordance with this curious persuasion that we are always writing to our congressmen. And monitoring the parleys of statesmen by mass frowns or mass nods of approval. And taking delight in the periodic hiring and firing of the cooks. Everyone tells us, and we are naive enough to believe, that we have done something wonderful (like holding aloft the torch of liberty, or exercising a great democratic franchise) when we cast a ballot for one of several candidates who are as indistinguishable as competing detergent powders.

Furthermore, we must always be poking around the stove to see what's cooking (the price of liberty is eternal vigilance). This is not a case of superiors keeping a watchful eye on their charges, but of the governed checking on the governors.

As middlemen we have the eggheads, the sociologists and survey-conductors. They are not cooks, but yolky busybodies, who take it upon themselves to probe the will of the common egg, so as to advise the cooks (in an unofficial but threatening capacity) how the eggs want the omelette turned.

So help me, children are even asked to advise on how their parents should bring them up. So why shouldn't students decide on their own curriculum, and constituents tell their representatives how to vote on every bill?

I know of a group of Catholics who met at regular intervals to hear lectures. The founding idea was that the men were to benefit from the wisdom and/or inspiration of the speakers. After several years the audiences had become lecturer connoisseurs.

They sat in judgment on every speaker, recording (on printed questionnaires) critical appraisals of his delivery, the content of his speech, his ability to hold their interest, his appearance and his timing. This information was hastily collated and dispatched to the Chapter in the next town, where again nothing said by the lecturer was received with an eager mind or a docile disposition.

Now don't take all this to mean that I am against democracy or voting.

This isn't democracy, it's a form of madness. It's an inversion of the proper order of reality. If you want a political term, it's mob rule.

More tellingly, it's a way of using a lot of energy, seemingly in the direction of good, which involves no actual practice of virtue. No moral transformation, on the part of those who use it. It's an effort to change the world without changing oneself. Such eggs ignore their own want of freshness.

We ought as a general principle to take a dim view of any project, however difficult it may be in other respects, which does not demand for its execution, some sacrifice or exercise of virtue on our part.

Minding someone else's business falls in this category.

On the other hand, minding one's own business always involves moral effort, which is why this is the precise, obvious and primary contribution which each person can make to the social omelette.

Let us take the child as a prototype.

For the child, to mind his own business would be to stop doing just as he pleases. It would mean that instead of criticizing his parents he would begin to obey and respect them. By our present assumption his are not perfect parents, so this might be hard. But neither are they monsters from whom the state has to rescue their offspring, so it wouldn't be impossible.

Suppose the child starts obeying. A peg has dropped into the right hole. This can be the beginning of an internal, probably painful, movement toward self-perfection on the part of the child. Furthermore, an opportunity is created for parents to improve as parents, since they now have the expectation of obedience. A whole segment of domestic wrangling ceases.

Should there be a widespread movement toward obedience among children we might even be spared TV and magazine interviews with adolescents in which offspring pontificate on their parents' ability in child rearing. How late should we be allowed to stay up? Is strictness or laxity a better policy? How can parents gain a more sympathetic understanding of teenagers? You know how it goes. An upsurge in the practice of obedience would permit these decisions to be left to the ineptitude of the adults, while the kids get on with their homework.

There are those who will say it is too much to ask a child to obey today's parents (or wives to be subject to today's husbands, or citizens to show respect to today's politician-statesmen, or students to respect today's teachers, or enlightened modern men to accept revelation).

It may be a lot to expect, but it's not too much considering the help that comes from grace.

And not too much since there is no real alternative. Can we quarrel with the order of the universe? The longer we put off the day of reckoning the worse it will be when it comes.*

---

* We could not find the rest of this article in the archives.

16

He Should Have
His Head Examined
AUGUST 24, 1958

"**I**S SAECULUM VERY SICK, DOCTOR?"
"Gravely ill."
"But he has so much energy!"
"It's feverish energy. I think he should have his head examined. Take him to Dr. Sapiens."
"After giving Saeculum certain routine tests, Dr. Sapiens shook his head."
"He's suffering from multiple confusions and recurrent blackouts. He can't think straight."
"Do you have in mind the birth control controversy in New York?"
"That's a good recent example of his mental confusion. You will recall that a doctor in a public hospital prescribed contraceptives for a diabetic Protestant woman, on the grounds that another pregnancy would endanger her life. The health commissioner refused to allow it, and a public controversy followed, with the Protestant Council and various liberal Jewish bodies aligned against what they considered to be sectarian Catholic influence."
"Yes, I remember. The Protestants made an official statement to the effect that Christian morality derives from Christian compassion—whatever that means."
"It's an unfortunate expression. They probably mean that for them it's not morality but compassion that's involved,

and that they feel sorry for this woman who is in danger of death."

"Is she in danger of death?"

"No, but she may be later, *providing* she gets pregnant again, and *to the degree* that diabetes places her life in jeopardy. The doctors acknowledge the double contingency when they say contraception is indicated by preventive medicine."

"Still, from reading the papers you get the emotional impression that it's a case of death or artificial contraception."

"You do. As though she were in danger of death, and as though artificial contraception were the only way to avoid pregnancy."

"Would it be fair to sum it up by saying that our Christian compassion is being evoked on the grounds of this one real hardship: that a woman and her husband need to practice (in *sickness* and in health) periodic continence?"

"Yes, on the surface it is an unfair representation. However, rarely (or why would this one be used as a test case?) problems of this sort do represent a serious choice and do call for much compassion. The point of confusion is the substitution of compassion for morality, whereas it should supplement morality."

"You said the patient had blackouts."

"Yes, we have an example in the same case. What's really at issue here is the morality of artificial contraception. If there is no morality involved, why shouldn't the woman take advantage of the easiest and surest method of preventing pregnancy?"

"Where does the blackout come in?"

"In this way. Artificial contraception is not only wrong but it is clearly and demonstrably wrong. Now the reasons why it is wrong have been explained again and again to the Planned Parenthood people and their followers among the liberal sects. But they cannot see it."

"You mean it's a subversion of God's purposes as written in the nature of human beings and of sex?"

"Yes. They usually avoid this particular point (it probably means nothing to them) and then misrepresent the whole explanation. They agree that sex is obviously for the continuation of the species. But this does not mean (as they like to intimate it does) that there are not accompanying benefits of health and happiness. Nor does it mean (as they persist in claiming it does) that human sexuality has to be exercised to its full biological capacities."

"Isn't this confusion rather than blackout?"

"It's both, really. The point I am making is that there it is, clear as day, and they simply do not see it."

"Then you think they are in good conscience?"

"Many of them probably are. Here is what I think: they are suffering from a disease called Spiritual Blindness. They probably inherited it from their fathers and grandfathers, who were brainwashed by scientific enlightenment and what was called the Higher Criticism of the Bible. Spiritual Blindness is a real blindness, of the intellect of course. It doesn't mean their minds are defective, but that the natural light by which we all see truth has been withdrawn from their minds."

"By whom and why?"

"By God, and as a punishment for unbelief. But as I say, the burden of culpability probably belongs to their grandparents."

"Is there any cure, Doctor?"

"Humility."

17

Mediation: New Style and Old Style

AUGUST 31, 1958

THESE DAYS THE WOMEN'S MAGAZINES ARE full of case histories from the marriage counseling files.

First the husband will tell his grievances. Then the wife will explain why she can't stand it any longer.

Next we get the diagnosis of the marriage doctor, who is usually a high echelon social worker, or a psychiatrist.

Of course there is fault on both sides, but there is always one culprit, one of the partners who has to be radically changed. This is often the very spouse who seemed wronged in the beginning, and his or her trouble is likely to be infantilism or some other sort of immature dependence.

Then, in the better magazines, we get the prognosis: this month's marriage will be saved because Mrs. Never-Grew-Up agrees to submit to treatment: last month's marriage is doomed because Mr. Tied-to-Apron-Strings refuses to cooperate with the counselors.

Let us set aside for the moment the amoral approach to marriage here exemplified. This is largely a matter of euphemisms anyhow. In the secular lexicon, "immature" or "negative," as applied to conduct, mean that the conduct is reprehensible.

Let us concentrate instead on the very limited ability of these secular counselors to deal with life's troubles.

The weakness of their approach is evident not just in marriage counseling: it runs through the whole field of what might be called the sociological-psychological approach to human affairs.

First of all, note that these human relations doctors insist on dealing with both contestants. If there is a disturbed child they must see the parents too. In marital troubles both husband and wife have to come to the clinic. Where there is group friction, there must be group therapy. In order to resolve the personality problems of the You Name It Company, the human relations engineers must be allowed to pry on the entire organization.

Next observe that our "fixers" have only one method of operation. First they spot the trouble maker. Then they bring him into line or get rid of him.

To sum up, their entire program of right in human relations rests on artificially contrived vantage points, and on the cooperative good will of those who are wrong (and least likely to cooperate).

Where they are not in a position to foster *mutual* understanding, all they can offer the innocent party is an understanding of the hopelessness of his situation.

If the sinner won't listen to them, they have nothing to say to him who is sinned against.

Back of it all is the conviction that the way to reform the world is to change the bad people.

At first glance, this seems obviously true. But is it? Why is it then that all these people who are so anxious to help with our problems really have no authority? They are not parents who can knock their quarrelling childrens' heads together and enforce discipline. They are not judges dealing with law breakers.

Now I submit that, outside of childhood and the law courts, outside also of situations which border on the medical or abnormal, the way to reform the world is to work through the good people. This is also the natural way, since it is usually the good person (the wronged person) and the good person only, who seeks help or who tries to do something about it on his own. No contrived hearing of both sides is necessary, nor is it usually possible.

Furthermore, this is the way of Christianity. The very fact that counselors don't know what to do with the person who is in the right, shows how narrowly they view this vale of tears and how far they have travelled away from Christian thinking.

To get the correct perspective here, we must see that the Redemption (which is the radical antidote to our human troubles and frictions) was the work of the Perfect Man. Christ was also God, of course, but it was on account of His human perfection that He was the *unblemished* victim of His own sacrifice. His method was immolation; the human contribution to His redemptive power was innocence. The fruit of His action was God's help for sinners.

Echoing Christ are the saints, whose vast power to change the world for the better again comes through their high degree of perfection.

So why shouldn't we imitate this pattern as well as we can on our own lower level?

If one person in a quarrel is relatively innocent and anxious to do the right thing, why not point out that the right thing is immolation? Why not suggest the heroic endurance of a bad bargain? Why not recommend a charitable love of one's tormentor? Why not encourage cheerfulness in the now one-sided making of sacrifices?

If Mr. Brown refuses to hear that he has a fixation, why not let Mrs. Brown in on the secret that her marital difficulties only *look* like a problem in human relations? Why not show her that, more deeply and more truly, they are the Cross?

18

A Saint for Televiewers
SEPTEMBER 14, 1958

THE POPE HAS MADE ST. CLARE THE GUARDIAN of television because she once, miraculously, saw things happening at a distance. So she is really the patroness of TV in its aspect as a scientific marvel.

There is another saint whom I suggest as a fitting patron for TV *viewers*. He is St. Alipius; pupil, friend and companion of the great St. Augustine. The two were born in the same town, received into the Church together, and afterwards were both consecrated to the African episcopate.

As a youth, my candidate patron had a great bent toward virtue, but developed a passion for the idle spectacles of the Circus, especially the gladiatorial shows. One day, just by chance, Augustine spoke about slavery to the Games, in a lecture at which Alipius was present. Alipius took the words personally and to heart. He resolved never to go again.

He kept his resolve until a day when some friends insisted he accompany them to a gladiatorial contest. He refused. He even said that if they forced him to go, he wouldn't look. So they took him there by force and he shut his eyes. But when he heard the crowd roar he opened his eyes just to learn the cause, intending to close them again quickly.

Anyone who has ever turned on TV "just to see" (if there is anything good on, or how the reception is tonight) knows what happened to Alipius. By his curiosity he fell. What he saw was that one of the combatants had been wounded.

Alipius became drunk with the rest of the crowd at the sight of blood. He shouted, he gloated, he fell into a sort of madness, and he relapsed into his former passion.

Not all the diversions offered by the Circus were violent (like our crime shows and wild west episodes). Some were innocent (like our innocuous TV entertainment) and some indecent (for which we also have counterparts).

It was the obsession for watching, rather than the nature of the spectacles watched, that chiefly harmed Alipius in the years that followed this episode. He went about his duties, but he lived as though under a cloud, which prevented any real fruition of his life. Before he had been dragged to that amphitheatre by his friends he had been on the road to conversion to Christianity. As a result of what happened that day, he did not enter the Church until he was freed from his obsession, by God's grace, many years later.

The reason I suggest the patronage of Alipius is obvious. We have in our own homes an instrument of far greater hypnotic power than the ancient circuses. The first problem of TV is *not* the separation of the wheat from chaff (as though we could watch harmless programs to our hearts' content), but the danger of obsession. A passion for watching TV can do to us what it did to Alipius; stultify and block any self-direction in living, especially in the matter of high goals and idealism.

The obsessed go through the motions of daily living, but that extra push, that deeper motivation, is no longer there. Continuously in the back of their minds is the anticipation of watching again as soon as possible, and naturally all their leisure is eaten up by the wonder screen in the darkened room.

Of course the TV obsession can do its greatest harm to youth. This is not only because children are in their most impressionable years, but because they ought to be doing something else with that wasted time, for which the opportunity will soon be forever lost.

I guess I know all the parental approaches to the TV problem.

The one least likely to succeed is the "I'll go to the amphitheatre but I won't look" compromise which tripped up Alipius. "We'll buy a TV set, but we'll watch it seldom and only the good things." I have seen the most admirable Christian parents of splendidly disciplined children fall flat on their faces with this one.

In the end they all admit that it's easier to resist getting a set than to control its use. In some cases the set mysteriously gets broken and never gets fixed again. In others it is relegated to the porch or playroom, so that the parents, at least, will be spared its ceaseless din.

TV may be harder to control than to resist, but resistance presents some formidable problems.

It means a sacrifice for parents who themselves want to watch TV, and there are always a few programs — news, great plays or favorite comedians — which make TV desirable. I know several parents who are completely happy without TV, but they are people with cultural, intellectual or spiritual resources far beyond the average.

Then there is the argument that it is bad to deprive your children of what is normal for the children of our time. It makes them "outsiders" to their own age. Their whole generation will learn to take TV in its stride, while they are warped in their youth by its deprivation and too powerfully influenced when later they can freely gaze.

This argument has some weight. I once knew a Frenchman who worked in New York and kept his family in Montreal. He explained that his children had not developed an immunity to the American Way of Life, including TV, and he didn't dare expose them to it. The South Sea Islanders who died on first exposure to our common cold provide a horrible example in the physical order.

So I guess you might as well have TV in your home if the pressure of juvenile conformity is crushing your kids and if you can't come up with something pretty exciting to fill the vacuum.

But if you can keep a fighting distance from the mob spirit, and if you have high aspirations for your children and some plans to help them on the way, then I suggest you use the argument from weakness. Instead of pretending you are strong enough to live with the thing, admit you are not. Explain that TV is indeed wonderful, but *we are so weak* we don't dare have a set in our house or we would have it on all the time. And how, then, would we ever get done all those other wonderful things we have planned to do for God and each other?

And pray to St. Alipius.

19

How to Overcome Your Background

SEPTEMBER 21, 1958

H AVE YOU EVER HEARD A SELF-MADE MAN berate his son?

"Why, when I was your age..." he begins, and goes on to claim that he made his millions, or got in Who's Who, or rose to the Board of Directors, because he worked long hours, or went to night school, or saved every penny, or whatever it was that he did when he was young.

It is clear to everyone except the old man that if Junior followed the parental pattern Junior would never make Who's Who or the Board of Directors, but the reason for this is not so universally clear.

Basically it is not because Junior is made of softer stuff. It is because the rising tide of public utilities, modern advertising, automobile manufacture, radio, trade unionism, or whatever it was that swept papa (or grandpa) into wealth and prominence, has virtually reached a stationary peak.

Sure, papa walked four miles each way to school, or broke ice to wash his face. Sure, he put in a 10 hour day in a 6 day week for $5.00. Sure, he was jailed three times for picketing. But the main reason for his success was an accident of circumstance. Shakespeare noted that some men are born great, some achieve greatness, and some have greatness thrust upon them. The self-made men of America belong almost entirely to the last group, because they were democratic citizens of a rich and swiftly developing country.

Papa was born in a small midwestern town of poor but pillar-of-America parents. All he had to do was take his rugged enthusiasm to the nearest city and grow along with it.

Or he was an Irish immigrant hod carrier with several strong brothers, just at the dawn of the great era of construction.

Or he was a Jewish sweatshop worker, who had but to persevere in organizing the union to obtain a country estate with a private swimming pool for his children's children.

Or he was the son of impecunious Protestant missionaries in India or China, who breathed in a knowledge of the Far East and of oriental languages while his contemporaries in America were suffering the Jazz age. Long after he had ceased practicing the religion which was its occasion, this cosmopolitanism served him well in the journalistic field.

Or he was of just the vintage at Yale which had only to take seriously the matter of increasing the sales of chewing gum to become in no time founder of a great advertising agency, raking in the millions.

Try it now! Try any of these now!

To have greatness thrust upon you today, you should have taken the precaution to be born Indonesian, Chinese or African Negro, with the addition, perhaps, of a Western education of some sort.

The rising tides have passed halfway around the world. Many people agree with Bishop Sheen's recent remarks in Brussels: that power, wealth and greatness of civilization are passing from the West, and that the great cultures of the future will develop in the East.

Whether or not this will happen, it is certainly true that American youth is not presented with almost automatic paths of success. Now you had better be born great, or at least with that sort of calculating ambition which will push you ahead of your equals or betters.

However, I would like to pose another problem. Suppose it is true that we live in the splendid decadence of a civilization which has seen its day, how are we to accommodate ourselves in this situation? Specifically, what goals are there for us and our children?

I think first we should note that what we have here in America is not just the brilliance and luxury of an over-ripe civilization. There is still another of those rising tides around. Call it a tidal wave, because it is all-engulfing. Just follow the path of least resistance and you will be part of it.

What is it? Where is it going?

It's the rising tide of collectivism. Just get on it with the rest of the crowd and you are likely to end up in perdition. You don't even have to be bad, just mediocre and passive. In this way you will put yourself beyond the possibility of controlling your own destiny, and there will be plenty of opportunity later for the compromise if you will. Because you know who will be calling the tune.

Okay, what is the alternative?

Transcendence. Or to put it more bluntly, be a saint. Live in other terms.

What Christian cares, really, if the power of this world passes to people with slant eyes and olive complexions? If that is what God wants, so let it be. That doesn't wipe us all out, or mean that God doesn't care about our souls.

But it does narrow down our earthly choices, and even more so those of our children. We might have liked them to work out a nice harmony between big shot and servant of God; movie magnate maybe, protecting morals and making millions.

If about now somebody ran a contest based on the best answer to the question: "Why should I bring up my child to be a saint?" the prize would go to those who said, "Well, I guess there is no alternative."

There seems to be no other form of greatness open to us Americans. Even though the world is clamoring for scientists, that tide is no longer in its modest beginnings, and you had better be a genius or you will surely be one of a multitude of routine workers.

But anyone, though he hails from the worst little out-moded puddle, can be a saint.

When the Roman Empire had reached a far worse state of decadence than the Western powers have now, there lived in it a teacher of rhetoric. He was a more refined and intelligent version of Dale Carnegie, teaching men to speak persuasively. He barely managed to support himself.

But then he became a Catholic, and a priest, and a bishop, and above all a saint, and he was greatness itself. Though the barbarians were coming in the doors and windows, he found more than enough work to do during his long life.

The civilization died, as had been predicted.

But for almost a thousand years afterwards the world, even humanly speaking, supported itself on the shoulders of that former teacher of rhetoric: St. Augustine.

20

Why Married Women Work

SEPTEMBER 28, 1958

W E MAY AS WELL FACE THE FACT THAT IN this crass world the upper hand belongs to the holder of the purse strings.

The things a really rich man can't buy are pretty well hidden in the spiritual realm. As a current example, the two contenders for Governor in New York State (Harriman and Rockefeller) are both multimillionaires, and neither was forced to accept candidacy by spontaneous popular clamor.

To bring the truth closer to home, observe how fortunate and rare are the parents who can exact obedience from an adolescent offspring without making some sordid comparison of their purchasing power with his.

And so it is with marriage. In the theoretical and normal situation both husband and wife work, but only one gets a pay envelope. He is head of the house.

Of course he is supposed to be head of the house in the nature of things we know that. Here we are only explaining how it came about that married women work (outside the home, and for money).

Like bosses and kings, husbands have their failings. It is not always a pleasure for a wife to be subject to her spouse. The less perfect and competent he is, the less perceptible is the pleasure. That's why men need to hold the purse strings; it reinforces their theoretical authority with tangible power.

Here we have one of those "unfair" dispensations of Providence with which feminists have long been doing battle. This is a battle that they have won.

I can remember how things were before the emancipation. My mother's friends would gather for tea and gossip (they all had maids or grown children so they weren't outdoing their husbands in drudgery). Nobody specifically said so, but little pitchers with big ears definitely got the impression that all wives were better and wiser than all husbands, and that the superior sex really ran the home, through flattery and other forms of indirection ("Make him think it's *his* idea...")

It was years before I realized that these women were really bolstering their own egos. They may have maneuvered many a little scheme, but in major matters they were right under the unpleasant domination of the Lord of the Manor. They knew it and they were chafing under it, but they were stuck. The key to their intolerable subordination was that he controlled the money.

Now that the feminists have triumphed, we can all see that money was indeed the clue to the situation. Today we have a quite different sort of marriage: the 50-50 partnership. Decisions are made *together*. *Housework* is also done together. And he and she leave together in the morning for the office or factory.

It was no easy transformation. In the old days there were no attractive and important openings for women in the business world. Widows had a rough time of it in taking in laundry or soliciting magazine subscriptions. There are still restricted areas and impregnable fortresses, but most of the professions have given way, and business has come to respect and remunerate vast hordes of females.

Matters have so far progressed that now the working world is making its own catastrophic adjustments, basing its salaries on the supposition that there are two adult breadwinners in the house. Or where the presumption is not official, it is noticeable in social pressure. The Jones are expected to live on an income roughly one and two-thirds that of Mr. Jones.

This makes it particularly hard on women who have approached the situation from the opposite direction. Their experience has been, not with domineering husbands, but with a long, ever-since-high-school-or-college servitude in the bureaucratic salt mines. They are sick of offices and business machines; of file cabinets and time clocks. They long to lord it over a three-room apartment and a couple of preschoolers, to use their feminine instincts and talents, and to control their own office breaks. But now even their husbands expect them to hold down an outside job.

It's a dilemma I don't propose to solve. What interests me here is the difference a little Christianity makes, or would have made.

Remember how the Church says that wives should obey their husbands as *Christ?* (and that husbands should love their wives as Christ loves the Church, but that is the other side of the coin, which we are not now considering). It seems like a small matter, this enhancement of man's natural headship in marriage by the Sacrament of Matrimony, but it makes all the difference. It removes the onus from a wife's position.

What if her husband is stupid and domineering? She can look past him to the Christ Whose Will she is doing. It's like a nun obeying a religious superior who is not the best of all possible religious superiors. Or like Peter obeying Nero.

Or, for that matter, it bears a marked resemblance to Christ's own obedience to His Father's Will in submitting to the unjust condemnation of the Jews.

I think that if the world had not first been secularized, we would not have seen women invading offices and factories, and that this would have been all to the good. Especially for the women themselves.

But now what?

I suppose it would be too much to ask that husbands be given back their authority, and never mind who earns the money. Or, as long as we are supposing, let's make it too much to ask that husbands also be given the money earned by the wives.

Too much, perhaps, but in the abstract a good way to right the situation. If a job nets the wide nothing: no equal status in the family council, no freedom to buy the extra luxuries she pleases, what sensible woman is going to keep on working, except for reasons of absolute necessity?

21

We Privileged Few

OCTOBER 5, 1958

I T DISTRESSES ME WHEN CATHOLIC SOCIOLO-
gists speak of us Catholics as a "minority group."

Is salt a "minor ingredient"?

Is yeast "struggling for existence"?

Is light on a par with anything else in the world?

When Catholics are called a "minority group" it implies
that there is some basis of similarity on which they as a
body can be compared with other social bodies, larger or
smaller. This is not the same thing as saying that there
are fewer Catholics than non-Catholics in the United States,
which is a perfectly legitimate numerical observation.

Here is what I think is the trouble:

Sociology is the science of society—of natural, human
society. Now the thing that binds Catholics together as a
group is precisely that they belong to another, superhuman,
divine society. So if you compare Catholics as a group with
social groups whose principle of unity lies in some human
social factor, like ethnic origin or the size of their pay
envelopes, see what you are doing. You are presuming a
common basis of comparison which you don't in fact have.
You are taking a divine society and treating it as though
it were a human one.

Of course it is true that Catholics also live in human
society, but it is not a human principle which unifies them
as a group. And you cannot ignore this supernatural principle of unity without destroying the unification.

As this whole matter is difficult to grasp, it will be useful to make a rough comparison. When a man dies, his soul leaves his body. This soul was the principle of unity in the living, human whole. The body looks the same for a while after death, but it would be an error to consider it as a physical unit, because the principle of unity has gone. And presently the body will disintegrate for this very reason.

On account of an analogous situation, sociologists ought to separate the Catholic body into its human constitutive elements before they begin their studies, since they are going to prescind from the transcendent principle of unity. Let them treat Italian Catholics as part of a group labeled "Italian," and Catholic factory workers as part of a group labelled "factory workers."

Otherwise they will come out with false findings or implications.

An example of such an error is the "minority group" idea. The expression "minority group" is loaded. It doesn't mean just that we are few in numbers. It means that we are in some sort of position of inferiority in society by reason of the fewness of our numbers. As a matter of fact, sociologists go so far as to talk about the "struggle for survival" that this minority group status entails.

Yet Christ has represented the matter of our being members of the Church completely differently. He was speaking specifically of our relationship to human society when He spoke of salt and leaven. What He said was that (regardless of whether we are few or many—yeast expands to leaven the whole mass, and only a pinch of salt is needed to savor a whole dish) we come bearing gifts. We are the white hope of the rest of society because of the new life which enters society through us.

Our relationship to society is apostolic, even when we are shedding our blood in testimony of the truth. It is never defensive in the negative sense of being wholly subject to superior numbers or strength.

Another example of erroneous conclusions arises in connection with our tenacious views on certain social doctrines such as divorce and artificial birth control.

Parenthetically, these are not Catholic views, but stem from the natural law. However, we are pretty much alone in holding them today, and we do so because we are guided by the authoritative teaching of the Church.

Now the sociological treatment of this situation is to put it on the neutral level of disagreement and percentages. Our doctrines are different from those of the majority of Americans. From this it follows that we are fighting for survival, because naturally it is hard to live in a society which is geared to other laws and customs.

How different the matter looks if we introduce the question of whose views are true! And what right have the sociologists to bypass this question? Once it is allowed to enter, we see ourselves as clinging to the truth in a sea of error. It is society which is threatened by perverting its very structure. On the other hand, we are struggling to save it from itself.

We said at the beginning of this column that *Catholic* sociologists have no right to see us as a minority group, which is exactly how we look to those outside the Church. That doesn't mean that Catholics can't be sociologists, but just that when they deal with the Church they have to take into account the special knowledge they have through revelation.

Similarly, a Catholic psychologist could not try to analyze Our Lord's character as though He were a mere man. And a Catholic historian has to see the incarnation as the focal point of even human history.

If Catholic scholars, or we ourselves, see human affairs exactly as non-believers see them, we are either weak in faith or bottling up our faith in narrow religious confines. If we look and feel more like a minority group than the salt of earth, the reason is not numerical. It is because our savor is low.

22

Little Man, What Now?
OCTOBER 12, 1958

(Original Editor's Note: *Readers sometimes ask how they can contact Mrs. Robinson. The address is Watch Hill Farm, Watch Hill Road, Peekskill, New York, and Mrs. Robinson will welcome your comments.*)

ABOUT THE TIME SAINT THÉRÈSE WAS WORK-ing out her way for little souls to attain heavenly heights, the socialists were predicting their scheme for little people to rise to wordly power. In retrospect it almost seems as though God sent us a child with an anti-dote for the poison we were about to drink.

Recall the setting: In the economic sphere, the 19th century furnished in real life the sort of hell-bent-on-profi t-and-the-devil-take-the-mere-employee sort of capitalist that is now only ranted about. He was a man of average virtue whom industrialism and sundry other factors greatly tempted to profiteer at the expense of a lower class which was without productive property and completely at his mercy. Mostly he yielded.

It was the socialists who first set about persuading the victims of this ogre's avarice that, pitiful though they were individually, they would have a lot of power if only they would unite and stand firm in withholding their indis-pensable labor until certain demands were met. More and more demands, as it turned out.

Something similar was going on in the world of ideas. The really "smart" men were atheists. Like the capitalists, they found themselves in absolute possession, despising faith and adoring science. But unlike the capitalists they had nothing in particular to gain from bothering about the minds of the little men. So in this field the little men whose faith had survived the French Revolution and the Reformation, had merely to lie low and confine their devotional lives within a narrow family circle. It was Saint Thérèse, whose own family led just such a withdrawn life, who showed men how to make great spiritual capital out of restricted circumstances.

The third factor in this situation was the Church. Full of wisdom as always, but excluded from public affairs and influence as never since her early centuries, she spoke — but few men listened.

We have been given a picture of the long, lingering look which Leo XIII cast after the 15-year-old Thérèse Martin who had just petitioned him to allow her to enter the Carmel before her next birthday. And it was this Leo who straddled the two sorts of impotence to which the little man had been reduced. He told the working man to use the only force which was available to him, numbers; but he warned that such action would improve nothing in the long run if it were not accompanied by moral reform.

Now some three quarters of a century later, we can weep if we will, because Leo's advice went unheeded in its secondary, but essential part. The labor movement has about run its course. It was not accompanied by moral reform, so it was largely a socialistic course. Trade unions are presently triumphant and are dictating the course of industry.

Most people rejoice at labor's victory. They see the worker protected on all sides like a fullback. They see his fair pay envelope, his short hours of work, and the lack of deference with which he quits work irresponsibly at the blow of a whistle. They note his bourgeois standard of living, the fancy car he drives. They realize that his swimming pool is not as big as the one belonging to the factory owner, but they know that it is his trade union, and not the factory owner, which calls the tune.

What they do not see, because their eyes like his are fixed on material gains, is that he has taken on the capitalist's vices while shedding some of his own virtues. He is ready to milk the capitalist dry and even, in his shortsightedness, to kill the factory that is laying the golden eggs. His sympathy for the downtrodden in other industries and countries does not go so far as to detract from his own prosperity. His treasures are no longer in heaven, now that he has found so many here. His goal is the infinite goal of avarice, which recedes as it is approached.

It need not have been so.

If there had been concomitant moral and social reforms, the little man might not now be in virtual possession of the earth, but he would be happier, and his security would come from the stability of society rather than from forced guarantees which jeopardize the whole social structure.

If the little man had only aspired to greatness in sanctity his trade organizations would not have had the burden of his materialism, his envy, and his desire for revenge. They would have worked for wages high enough to ensure decency and modest comfort, not luxury. They would have asked for a little more so a man could save to own a little property. They would have made vast efforts to reconcile owners and workers on a basis of love and common interest, rather the hardening of their antagonism into class warfare. They would have eschewed the triple goals of more and more money and leisure and security: Instead they would have worked for wages geared to families and to degrees of skill, for conscientious work in return for fair pay, and for the workers' sense of responsibility to the common good.

The early days of Jocism* saw a deeply spiritual, yet practical, approach to improving the condition of the workers.

---

* In reference to the movement founded by Fr. Joseph Cardijn receiving papal approbation by Pius XI (in 1925) to work for the reconciliation of the Church with the industrial workers of the world.

And Martin Luther King has recently edified us with his spiritual-practical approach to another social problem.

But here in America it is too late either to infuse spiritual influence into the workers movement, or to use this movement as a ladder of charity. The sacrifices have long since been made (not usually by us Christians), and the purely material battles won. You could never convince *me* that it was now my serious Christian duty to attend routine union meetings or to get help on parliamentary procedure, even in the faint hope of getting rid of communist leadership. As the unions stand they are socialistic, so why shouldn't the socialists run them? We lost that battle; let's forget about it.

But we haven't lost the war. Let's cast around for a terrain more favorable to the use of our own weapons.

23

Good Riddance
OCTOBER 19, 1958

W AY BACK IN PRE-TELEVISION DAYS THERE
was a radio comedian, now dead, named Fred
Allen. He had a keen natural wit and worked
hard to put on a different show every week. This is more
exhausting than changing audiences every week, as he
had previously done in vaudeville.

One night he announced that he had posted bond with
some lawyers down on Wall Street to guarantee recompense
for anyone who, by tuning in to Fred Allen's show, missed
his chance at the big money being offered by a rival show
on another network (one of those shows where they tele-
phone people at random).

I thought this was a big joke and that the comedian
was lightheartedly making fun of the American public for
its avarice. But he didn't sound lighthearted, and it turned
out to be a serious offer.

Now I wasn't much of a radio fan, and so I may have
drawn false conclusions. Nevertheless, I always thought that
Fred Allen's spirit was broken about then; that it was hard
for him to believe, and too hard for him to swallow, that his
fans should desert him for a mere quiz-giveaway program.

After that, and with the coming of television, quiz programs and contests and giveaway shows multiplied like
white rats. Some were vulgar, some had intellectual pre-
tensions, some were trivial; many, especially during the
daytime, featured housewives in a frenzy of cupidity over

showy gadgets and tawdry gifts. The communications marvel of the ages, the invention which had been hailed by the Pope himself as an incredible educational instrument, pandered day after day to what can only be described as the race track spirit in American living rooms. Nothing could stop it.

And now, overnight, quiz shows have become *persona non grata*. As they fade into oblivion, let us take an instructive look at them and at ourselves.

We were shocked to learn of the moral degeneration from which they died. Yet a little graft here and there is really not such a big step down for shows which represented the convergence of several streams of avarice. Quiz shows did the sort of thing with brains that Miss America contests do with beauty — exhibit them for profit.

From the showman's angle, they were a cheap way of getting non-professional talent. Just as there are beautiful girls who do not enter contests, so there are colorful characters who do not enter show business.

For the contestants they were manna from heaven, a sudden, startling and rather absurd way of getting rich overnight by playing children's games or by drawing on knowledge which had been acquired for its own sake. There were contestants naive enough to see in quiz shows a matching of wits; and in their popularity, a public thirst for knowledge. There was just enough of a tinge of this to give the illusion.

By and large we, their mass audience, were driven by the gambling spirit, vicariously sharing the tension of playing for high stakes. The contestants were our race horses, so they had to be appealing and the race had to be exciting.

That's why the quiz shows were fixed; to provide an interesting stable of contestants and to maintain the tension. Hardly any of the shows were phoney from beginning to end. The natural course of events was just manipulated when necessary.

Still, the whole business is a serious reflection on our declining morals.

The least shocking exposure is that showmen should go in for a little deceit, as that is almost their normal stock in trade. Still, this time it had considerable magnitude and was perpetrated with an unusually innocent air of integrity. And it carried with it the reputation of large manufacturers and networks.

There is really more to be shocked about with the contestants, as they are not normally in the show business. It is remarkable, for instance, that so many people found it no indignity to appear on the programs. The indignity which they didn't feel was especially apparent in the case of the housewives who almost swooned over merchandise. I know that women have strong acquisitive instincts, and that they characteristically act like an embattled mob at bargain sales, but I lament it, and I blush for my sex. Women should, like the Valiant Woman in the Bible, be competent in the material order, but only as a virtue connected with the loving care of their household, and this is not what it looked like on the giveaway programs.

Now let's get down to us who watched. We began by preferring a long chance at easy money to an evening's entertainment, and we continued in our mania until we found the game was crooked.

We too have imagined ourselves attracted to quiz shows for intellectual reasons. It is an easy matter to test.

If our church has had to resort to bingo and games-of-chance bazaars to raise funds, it was the gambling spirit. If we have deepened our reading lately, it was love of knowledge.

Well, it's over now, and good riddance. I see a long line of travelling gunmen appearing on the horizon. Which of our weak spots are they going to probe?

My guess is this: They are going to appease that thirst for heroism which we all have gnawing at us somewhere, and which finds no ready outlet in our humdrum, proletarian lives.

It's kind of a way of keeping the patient under sedation.

24

This is How it's Done
OCTOBER 26, 1958

I T SEEMS AS THOUGH EVERY TIME GOD GIVES us something hard to do He gives us another something to do which is easy and natural and which somehow imitates the hard thing.

He wants us to love Him in a filial way, so He gives us human fathers to show us what He means. "You have complete confidence in your father's love — all right, have this same sort of confidence in Me." "If you ask your father for bread, does he give you a stone? What makes you think I will?"

He asks us to love our neighbor, as ourselves, and he gives us marriage, in which the temporal fortunes of husband and wife are so inextricably identified that it might be one person instead of a pair, who gets richer or poorer, is honored or disgraced.

He has also asked us to love the sinner and hate the sin. Here again He has given us a special situation in which we naturally follow this injunction. We love our own children with a steady love, as manifest when we spank them as when we kiss them goodnight. It is when we spank them that we are hating the sin and loving the sinner.

Right away we can learn something from this homey model. We aren't just to hate sin in the abstract, as though we bore a grudge against lying. Lying doesn't exist without a prevaricator. No, we hate the sinner's sinning, and the reason we hate it is because it disfigures the one we love.

This leads us a step further. Our love for our children is not just an emotional response to their charm, but it is simultaneously a desire for their goodness and perfection. We love them whether they are good or bad; but with rejoicing when they are good, and with sorrow and corrective measures when they are bad.

Now that is just the way God loves us, with a steady but corrective love. He makes His sun to shine on the just and the unjust, but He also permits providential misfortune to fall on sinners for their repentance or betterment. Until that final day in Heaven when our perfection will allow us to be united blissfully with God, His love for us will continue to be warming and cauterizing in varying proportions.

Now our particular problem here is how to have the sort of love for our neighbors that we have for our children and that God has for us.

Fortunately we are not expected to do this by our own powers. The wonderful, built in capacity of parents to love even their repulsive children, does not carry over to the world at large. So we must borrow some of Our Heavenly Father's supernatural (to us) power to love even the most repulsive of men.

This borrowed power is, of course, charity. As it is the very same love that God has for us, it should enable us to love everybody (or rather, anybody—we don't know everybody) with a perfecting, corrective warmth.

Charity obviously does not accomplish this overnight. We keep wobbling from the sinner to the sin. In an effort to stir up love for our neighbor we tend to brush aside as unimportant his irreligion, mediocrity or vice. Then we go to the opposite extreme, get censorious, speak to him coldly, and in general make a mockery of our love. How will we ever reach an equilibrium?

Fortunately we have lately been given another model from whom to learn this science of loving sinners while hating sin: Pius XII.

A pope is like a human father, except that he has more children. But he is also like God, in that his is a supernatural fatherhood.

Pius XII was preeminently successful in his spiritual fatherhood. The whole world was amazed at the intensity and universality of his love for men. Yet he was the one man on earth whom everybody knew to stand undeceived and invincibly opposed to the forces of evil. He unhesitatingly and swiftly excommunicated Catholics who supported these forces.

We learn from his example that the reconciliation of love for sinners and hatred for their sinning takes place at the summit. Not at the peak of power, but at the peak of holiness, the point where sin is most clearly seen and charity is most intense.

We also get a glimpse of a deeper truth; that there is really only love, and that hatred stands in function of that love. The hatred of the sinner's sinning has to be there, even for God, until the object of love is perfected.

That is why it is such a terrible thing, such a deformation of love, to ignore the potential perfectibility of those we love. We see an example of this in parents who indulge and do not discipline their children. We see another example in contemporary thought. The world pleads with us to love people "as they are," or "for themselves." The world thinks that if we love them "in God," or "for the sake of God," we are somehow violating these sacred canons.

The opposite is the case. Unless we include God in our loving we will not have the power to love people who do not appeal to us. We will be loving a narrow circle of compatible or useful neighbors, not for their own sake, but for our own sake—for the pleasure or profit we get from it. Furthermore, when we love with charity we do love people as they truly are: imperfect and called to perfection. We see them on a journey to a great goal, and friendship demands we help them along the road.

Whom we help, and how we help them, depends on our circumstances and the prudence and capacity which we develop ever more and more through holiness. It may be prayer, or advice, or denunciation, or one of the works of mercy, or loaning a book, or some great social reform, or conversation at a party. The important thing at the beginning is to see the general obligation.

25

Culture and Such
NOVEMBER 2, 1958

ONE OF MY BEST FRIENDS CAN NEVER GET "I" and "me" straight.

There was a time when I tried to reach her. Everytime she said "I" when it should have been "me," I would quietly supply the correct case. Then we would go through sessions in which I would say, "When you are talking about Jane and me, leave out Jane and see how it sounds," Or I would explain about objective and nominative cases, transitive and intransitive verbs. It wasn't much help.

Nor did I much care. And when President Eisenhower, in some impromptu television remarks, said "for you and I," I decided my friend would be able to limp along in society despite her grammatical shortcomings, and gave up hounding her.

I have noticed several things relative to this subject of grammar.

One is the pendulum shift of the error.

Back in the old days the non-grammatical used "me" where they should have used "I." "It is me." "Me and Jimmy went to the races."

Now they use "I" when they should use "me." "He gave Johnny and I a dollar."

I see this shift as an uninformed groping for self-betterment. People got the idea that there was something vulgar about the way they used "me" and something elegant about using "I" more frequently, but since they didn't know the rules they just threw in "I" more or less at random.

What got me thinking about my friend's grammar was reading some more of the discussion that is going on about Catholic intellectuals, and how poor our showing is in the area of the mind. We don't have any Einsteins! We don't have any Tillichs! So far I have refrained from tossing my views into this controversy, but now I am moved to make a few personal observations.

I am not mortified by the Catholic lack of intellectual prestige, and one reason is because I attend Wellesley-in-Westchester kaffee klatches, where I observe at first hand the intellectual impoverishment of the non-Catholic mind. Here are women who speak perfectly grammatically, have reasonably high IQ's, and who are considered to have gone to one of the best colleges. They are charming besides, and seem to have good will. They know period furniture, gardening, current events, probably several languages and something about the arts. They do not know the truth about God, the Church, Jesus Christ, the natural law and the meaning of life. This ignorance of the things that really matter throws the whole of their lives off balance, distorts their judgment of a thousand things, and pinions their mental life to a superficial level.

The big agitation among Wellesley alumni these days is to raise some 15 million dollars to increase teachers' salaries. The theory is that better pay will attract better teachers, which will cause the standard of education at the college to soar even higher.

By an odd chance, this is exactly the remedy which Catholic colleges propose for their failure to turn out Einsteins.

Now, I went to Wellesley and I know that what is wrong with education there is totally irrelevant to the matter of faculty salaries. It may be that the teachers need more money, but this is a problem apart.

I am not familiar with Catholic colleges in the same way, but I would guess that the same thing applies. I'm sure their deficiencies are not the same as Wellesley's, but they are probably equally remote from the matter of teachers' salaries.

Perhaps, for instance, Catholic colleges are more concerned to turn out rocket engineers, for reasons of prestige (what other reasons would there be? We are racing all too fast in the direction of space), than to form Catholic minds in all students according to their capacities.

And this brings me back to Tillich. He's the big Protestant theologian who is now teaching at Harvard. He recently "made" the Saturday Evening Post. He is lauded as an original thinker of great influence. We wish we had his equal—or at least the Catholic breast beaters wish we had.

May I draw their attention to Frank J. Sheed, that indefatigable layman who has taught theology in season and out of season, indoors and out of doors, the length and breadth of our land, and who has in recent years been given a most extraordinary honorary degree in theology at the special request of the Holy See—so that no one can now doubt his merits as a theologian.

Of course Mr. Sheed hasn't made the Saturday Evening Post, but that is because he is too dogmatic. His orthodoxy also prevents his competing with Tillich as an original thinker. So his influence is limited to Catholic circles and to street corner crowds he occasionally addresses. But what multitudes of them! And what an important influence! A doctrine once explained by him is forever remembered.

By contrast, Tillich does not, in my studied opinion, believe in the God of Christianity. I consider this a devastating deficiency for a theologian. Using a Madison Avenue cliché, Tillich says that what religion in America lacks is "dimension in depth." By this he seems to mean that we don't *feel* deeply enough about religious type things. If you transpose his theme into the Christian framework which is not his, it would simply mean that there is a lot of religious enthusiasm and talk in America, but too little real holiness. This is true, but it is not a very profound or startling observation. This is something to ponder: that the simple truth sounds less exciting than its counterpart in the realm of half truth.

I guess the moral of these desultory observations is that a world bred in ignorance and scepticism honors only those whose brilliance remains within its set boundaries; and that those of us whose charitable duty it is to break down these boundaries in God's good time, must not covet the honors within, while we wait to bring the fullness of truth to our straying brothers.

26

Learning the Hard Way
NOVEMBER 16, 1958

T HERE ARE TWO WAYS TO LEARN THE GREAT
lessons of life: the Easy Way, and the Hard Way.

The Hard Way is through personal experience.
Thus you can learn by dying that the soul is immortal,
by "getting caught" that youthful steady-dating is risky,
by the electric chair that crime doesn't pay, by legalized
divorce the merits of monogamy, and by capitulating to
Russia the evils of Communism.

The Hard Way is always costly, and usually fatally so. Life
has few prodigals, and many who feed bitterly on remorse.

We are not meant to learn like this: The Hard Way exists
only as an alternate to the natural harmony between truth
(or right) and reality. What isn't true (right), doesn't work.
So obviously, we should concentrate on learning what's
true (right) and act accordingly.

But we Americans are pragmatic, which means we operate the other way around. "It's true if it works," we say.
And we are ready to try anything once.

Here lies the case for the conservatives among us. They
shudder whenever we destroy a tradition or an institution
which embodies the accumulated wisdom of generations.
They wept when Franklin Delano Roosevelt departed from
the gold standard for the shifting sands of manipulated
currency. They rent their garments when the Supreme
Court abandoned the standard of constitutionality for newly
hatched ideas of the good and the right.

Never mind the conservatives for the moment. There comes a time in these matters when so much of the foundation of society has been irreparably destroyed that the defense of what good remains is a rear-guard action, and the best forces should concentrate on laying a new foundation.

A new foundation does not mean novelty in the irresponsible way of the liberal iconoclasts. It means the embodiment of principles in contemporary circumstances, so as to build a new structure for society.

One of these principles is a system of legitimate authority which is properly respected, because this is the Easy Way in which God intended men should learn from the wisdom of others; others who are older, wiser, more learned, more responsibly placed than ourselves. We are not to judge their wisdom or prudence. We are to accept it.

Respect for authority is the operative virtue of the Easy Way.

We may as well face the fact that this respect has been largely lost.

Children have lost respect for their parents, colonies for the empires which gave them the benefits of western civilization, citizens for the law and the lawgivers, students for their teachers. Not entirely of course, but to an alarming degree.

The net result is that everyone is in danger of learning the Hard Way. Ex-colonials have to be swallowed up by Russia. Juvenile delinquents have to ruin their lives before they get well started on them, we have to invite the welfare state to rule over us before discovering that it destroys freedom.

So here is our problem: We have to make it possible again for people to follow the Easy Way. This means we must restore respect for authority. How?

Well, first we must realize that we are standing amidst the debris of a crumbling social structure. We must act as though we were starting anew (because we almost are) instead of mending a few leaks. It will do no good, for instance, for parents to command obedience, or to point out how right they are. They still are often right, but authority can't rest on proof of rightness. It must rest on the presumption of rightness.

In a word, it must rest on confidence.

Now confidence should rest in a person, or an institution, and not so much in what that person or institution does. So those in positions of authority must prove their worthiness, or their trustworthiness. And this proof will most easily be seen in the integrity which they themselves demonstrate, and in the sincerity of their interest in those whom they rule.

Finally, we should realize we are not living in an age of rebellion, however much superficial evidence we may see to the contrary. For everyone is looking for leadership, for authority in which to have confidence.

Ponder the case of De Gaulle in the political field.

But it is the same all the way up and down the scale.

27

Tests of Faith
NOVEMBER 23, 1958

A GOOD GAME FOR CATHOLICS TO PLAY IS:
"What would test your faith?"
The idea is for each person to tell what special study or scientific discovery, what current event or modern idea, tends to make him uneasy about his religious beliefs. It is a good game because it brings peoples' vulnerabilities into the open where they can be diminished, possibly with the help of the other players.

It's surprising how varied these weak points are.

The sight of the wicked prospering gave the Old Testament Jews a hard time, because it made them wonder if God really saw and appreciated their own righteousness. Now that we are less certain of our own virtue and more certain that rewards and punishment will be fairly meted out in the next world, we are less apt to question God about the moral quality of this world's greatness.

I know someone whose faith might waver at the elevation of unqualified prelates to positions of high responsibility in the Church. It would tend to shake his confidence in the guiding presence of the Holy Ghost.

My own faith will be tested the day medical research develops a pill to make bad people good people. I know it can't be done, and that no modification of our physical natures, however clever, can force our free wills, but just the same I mean to bone up on the body-soul relationship. The day the newspapers carry a plausible report that Dr.

So-and-So's chemical research on hamsters presages the obsolescence of jails, I mean to put my finger right on Dr. So-and-So's weak spot.

Interestingly enough, the converse situation has already arisen in brainwashing, which seems an invincible method of making good people into bad people.

Of course Faith is a supernatural gift and is increased by making acts of faith, but we must consider what it is that we have been given. Faith is a new intelligence. It is for knowing God and the truths of revelation. But this knowledge overflows into a new perspective on this life and the things of this world, so this new perspective can also be included in our act of faith. For instance:

O God. I believe everything the Church teaches, and in particular at the moment I believe that we are fallen creatures who stand in need of the grace that Christ has won for us. I therefore know it is nonsense to hold that men can become perfect, and perfectly happy, and get along harmoniously with one another if only society is rearranged on a classless basis and all power is given to the state. But, O God, I am being bombarded with this erroneous doctrine in various disguised forms, usually mixed in with truths about justice and injustice. Please strengthen my faith so that I may know which is which, and work toward a world pleasing to You.

Since Faith gives us this power to see things in God's perspective, we must use it, and not just wait for experts to write books on apologetics. The game of "What would test *your* faith?" is not for experts but for ordinary people. It's like adjusting your glasses.

Take, for example, the simple fact that many Catholics are bad people. Look at it from one side, and you will put a black mark up against the Church. Look at it from on high, and you will exclaim: "Yes, the Holy Ghost must be protecting this Church, or it would never survive the people who are in it."

I remember reading once that Saints Cyril and Methodius were not sent to the Slavs (whose apostles they became) purely as missionaries, but for quasi-political reasons. Ha! Mixed motives. The glories of Church history are once again revealed to be tarnished!

Not at all. Here is just another case of how God gets what He wants in spite of what we want, of God writing straight with crooked lines, as Claudel said.

A parallel instance is the conquest and colonization of Latin America, where God brought the Faith to millions, and raised up saints as early as the 16th century, through the instrumentality of adventurers and gold seekers.

The late Monsignor McMahon* of the New York Archdiocese could lift up the hearts of audiences by simply relating the facts of history as seen through the eyes of faith, without adding any pious exhortations. He loved to quote the papal statement that the Church needs no man's lies. His speciality was the nemesis, or kick-back, of history.

A perfect example of this nemesis is found in the sins of Pope Alexander VI, seen through the canonization of his great grandson, Francis Borgia. (God allows evil because of the greater good He means to draw out of it.)

Another is the full tale of Maria Monk, whose lurid, 19th century "revelations" about immoralities in a Canadian convent are to this day available in little blue books. Maria claimed to have been a postulant, I think, among nuns whom she accused of conducting themselves shamelessly, with the aid of underground passages to a nearby rectory. She gave minute descriptions of the convent to New York audiences of surprisingly respectable Protestants. Catholics raised money to send an investigating committee of leading citizens to Montreal. The convent turned out to be a House of the Good Shepherd, to which Maria had been sent by

---

* Monsignor Thomas J. McMahon (1909–1956), a priest of the Archdiocese of New York, he was National Secretary of the Catholic Near East Welfare Association from 1943 to 1955.

the courts. Nevertheless, the "disclosures" continued, even after Maria started bringing her illegitimate girl along to the platform with her.

Maria died in an asylum for insane paupers. Her daughter was sent to a Catholic orphanage, grew up piously, and afterwards married a rich man. When he died, she financed the building of a parish church (still standing today in the New York Archdiocese) in reparation for the sins of her mother.

28

Grouping and Groping
NOVEMBER 30, 1958

W E KNOW A YOUNG BOY WHOSE SCHOOL is a showcase for modern educational theories. For a long time we couldn't find out what grade he was in, apparently because it isn't very clear in his school where one grade ends and the next begins. The pupils call the teachers by their first names. There are no examinations, and I'd rather not know what they substitute for the old fashioned report card.

The main subject is always Core. This is an elaborate, corporate study of something the pupils could hardly avoid learning in the normal course. One year it was New York (all the students live there); this year it's How Men Live (in houses, by eating, etc.).

There is also something called Group. Not A Group, or The Group, or Group Study or Group Play; just Group. It turns out that this is Gymnastics.

Exercise is not the important thing, apparently (just as in Core, learning is not the important thing), but togetherness, or cooperation.

Let the readers of this column be warned against the current obsession with social adjustments, which extends far beyond the progressive schools.

Let them look with suspicion on anything called a group or a team which wouldn't have been called a group or a team circa 1900. It may be all right, but let it prove itself.

If they want my further advice, they will avoid like poison all those non-directive type gatherings which purport to iron out problems or arrive at truths by some mysticism of concerted effort.

The Great Books courses are of this sort. The leader of the group qualifies by abjuring leadership. Ideally he should say nothing, but he is allowed to stimulate discussion by provocative questions, and he must encourage silent members to speak, whether or not they have anything to say.

Owing to these courses, a lot of people have read a lot of classical writings; some full of wisdom, some riddled with error. As the readers had no criterion for deciding which was which, and as it is a point of honor for the leader not to enlighten them (if he knows!) they are rather worse off in the end than in the beginning.

It doesn't figure, until you understand what the group leader is groping for, and that this is not what the group members are groping for, nor what was held out to them as bait. The key lies in the operation of cross purposes.

Parents send their children to school to learn to read and write and a few other concrete things. But those who mastermind the schools consider study secondary to their own half-cocked experiments in group living. That's why they advance dull pupils in spite of their academic failures. And that's why they can't look at a gifted student without seeing him as deficient in well roundedness.

We simple-minded adults join Great Books courses to repair our ignorance. But the group leader wants less to feed our minds than to stimulate them, and if he is well trained in modern techniques, he has darker motives still, in the realm of welding together our purely fortuitous little gathering.

It's as though we, being hungry, came together to eat, only to find the cook intent on stimulating our appetites or manipulating the dinner conversation.

"We want you to THINK; we are not interested in WHAT you think." (Heavens, no, their democratic, pluralistic consciences are too delicate to pontificate about who and whether God is, or what constitutes right or wrong. They will only allow themselves to manipulate people.)

This THINK business was the battle cry when I was in college, but at that time there was still a pretension that we were thinking through to the truth. We were permitted to hope that the mind would finally find rest in its natural object, the truth. It was not a lively hope, considering how long our aging teachers had been beating the bushes in vain, but there was a lot of talk about Socrates setting out on his fragile bark. Though we might never reach it, truth was presumed to exist in some distant and luminous place beyond oceans.

Of course the reason truth eluded my college contemporaries was that they had turned their backs on it, and were hastening in the opposite direction. The comparison with Socrates was purely sentimental.

Since then things have gone from bad to worse, which is to say from implicit to explicit. The hope is gone, there is no absolute truth, and the search has become rather pointless. The downgrading of intellectual endeavor is the natural consequence.

The substitution of social adjustment for academic learning is the work of well meaning idiots. This is harsh, but it's true. At least it clears them; they know not what they do. But that is no reason why we shouldn't know what they are doing; not just the particulars, but the errors which give them rise.

They are trying to make us into social beings, to form us into groups which work cooperatively and harmoniously. It's a good idea, but they are a little late in coming up with it. God long ago had the same idea and wrote it in our natures. He even reinforced in various ways the groupings which He considered primary: the family, society, marriage, the Church. And (because He is an intellectual) He saw that a lot of people couldn't be a unity unless they all had some one purpose, or interest, or focus, or jeopardy, or need, which united them. In short they all have to grope for one same thing, which is the very reason why they are all brought together, and which is sometimes called the principle of unity.

Our masterminds have made the mistake of substituting a technique for the principle of unity. But once they have abandoned the principle of unity (and to put it in second place is as good as abandoning it) they have lost the unity. They will never restore it by controlled group discussion or simulated life situations.

29

Two Men, A Woman, and a Generation

DECEMBER 7, 1958

(Original Editor's note: I'm not sure I agree with all Carol Robinson has to say in this column but I think it a stimulating bit of thinking. Those clergymen who disagree — or agree — are invited to write Mrs. Robinson their views at Watch Hill Farm, Watch Hill Road, Peekskill, N.Y.)

B ILLY GRAHAM AND NORMAN VINCENT PEALE are the men; the woman is the journalist and columnist, Dorothy Thompson. There are two other people involved, but they are dead. Their names are Adam and Eve.

The Generation is that which is now aging; the local, Protestant American; the subject, Evolution. The purpose is to illustrate, by a classic case, the route of faith.

Even now Evolution is still only a theory. No one has yet seen one species evolve into another, and the evidence pointing to its having happened during the eons of pre-history is not conclusive. So we are free to suppose that it might have pleased God to create each successive gradation of life separately, to set the stage for man whom He then made out of the slime of the earth, breathing life into him and making him master of the material universe.

Or we can suppose that it might have pleased God to let the whole process germinate from the potentialities He placed in the first living cell, up to and including the matter from which the body of Adam was to be formed;

and that God breathed into the material for that body a rational, immortal soul, just as He has done for each one of Adam's descendants since.

We can be calm about Evolution now, but it first reached our shores as a "scientific certitude" that men were merely higher apes evolved by a process of natural selection. Along with other rationalistic doctrines (which will be omitted here for brevity's sake), it mocked the credulity of the Bible and sent much of Protestantism reeling. It had an unsteadying effect on Catholics too, but more in England than here, and the Pope took strong and swift measures to restore balance.

Perhaps you have wondered why there is sometimes so little difference that exists within a single denomination (such as high and low Episcopalians, the liberal and orthodox Presbyterians). It is largely because of the impact of Evolution and the other rationalist doctrines. Until this happened, Protestantism had been fissioning into sects, sometimes because of disputes about church government, but mostly because of minor doctrinal differences. But since the Bible was the standard of belief, however interpreted, and since the Bible was now said to be incompatible with scientific fact, all Protestants faced a common crisis which crossed sectarian borders.

Protestants had three alternatives to choose from; all of them unfortunate. Our two men and a woman can stand as representing them today. These people are not the end products of the choices, but rather the full flowerings of the warped goodness which each contained.

The three choices were: faith as against reason (Billy Graham); faith subordinate to reason or science (Norman Vincent Peale); and reason to the abandonment of Christianity (Dorothy Thompson). All three conceded at least implicitly, that faith and reason were now irreconcilable.

Those who made the first choice, the Bible Christians, were largely simple and/or uneducated people, who were not in any case particularly aware of the demands of reason, and that is why they were able to choose "irrational" belief in all sincerity. It is sincerity which has remained their mark, a particularly earnest sincerity in the case of Billy Graham. He preaches the Christian message straight (not quite full, but straight and uncompromising), and from revelation. He doesn't go on into theology, and therefore he is unable to make any but the simplest personal and domestic application of his religion to daily life. The narrowness and the oversimplification of Evangelism make it more and more inadequate to our complex world.

It is an ever-so-short step from an inability to cope with the temporal order, to a denial that Christianity cares about that order; from a disregard of history to an expectation that the world will end in the very near future. There must be many who cross the border of Evangelism into the camp of Jehovah's Witnesses.

Among the liberals, Norman Vincent Peale, a monumental extrovert and do-gooder, knows less theology than one would believe possible for a man of the cloth, but he doesn't have revelation to fall back on either. Dr. Peale has zeal, or perhaps we should just call it energy. He is a genuine product of liberal Protestantism; for those who made this second choice leaned toward active temperaments (that's why they number so many prominent businessmen and industrialists among their laymen) and practical minds, which could be content with a perfunctory religious practice. We owe to them the practice of religion as a "feeling," usually induced by hymn singing or organ music.

The irony of the liberal position is that it is based on a combination of religion and reason and winds up with neither. Dr. Peale is anxious to help everyone. He has a whole clinic full of psychiatric help for "people with problems," and he is full of advice himself. But all this activity, whether bad or good, has little to do with Christianity and may soon turn against it, as it often appears to do in his syndicated question and answer columns.

The mark of the third group, the ex-Protestant division, is high-mindedness and unrest. We see it in Dorothy Thompson, who has been a radical and iconoclast, who fought bitterly against Hitlerism, who has married three times (once to Sinclair Lewis), who has loved truth, and who is now at 63 a wise woman in almost all fields except one, but still not at peace.

She recently wrote a tribute to her late and much beloved artist husband, in which not once did she allow herself to hope for life and reunion after death. Yet she, like not a few of our prominent intellectuals and artists, was born a minister's daughter, and one can surmise from her general character that she never lost her nostalgia for religion and that the world of the spirit has a great attraction for her. It is probably this very fact which keeps Dorothy Thompson from reopening that door to Christian belief which she closed so long ago in an effort to preserve her intellectual integrity.

30

The Creedless Golden Rule

DECEMBER 14, 1958

O VER AND OVER AGAIN PEOPLE ASSURE ME they have no need for church going, for creed or sacraments; they simply live by the Golden Rule.

They seem to be under the impression that the Golden Rule can be separated from everything else Christ said and yet be considered the high point of His teaching. They also seem to consider it a comprehensive and definitive summation of the rules for Christian living.

In my opinion there is nothing so vague, so cursory, so barren of legitimate implications as the out-of-context admonition to do unto others as you would have others do unto you.

It does express a commonplace and superficial experience. When Mr. Jones loans his lawnmower to Mr. Smith, whose own has broken down at a moment crucial to good lawn care, Mr. Jones is apt to wave aside expressions of gratitude with "oh, think nothing of it. If I were in your spot, I'd be coming to you for help."

But let Mr. Jones make the mental calculation that now, with Smith in his debt, he can count on borrowing Smith's snowplow next winter, or that this gives him an opening to see Smith some insurance (Do unto others *so that* others will do unto you) and any similarity to virtue vanishes.

Or see what happens if you press it in another direction:

"I won't play around with Jones' wife, because I wouldn't like Jones to play around with my wife." This is several light years away from "I won't play around with Jones' wife because God has forbidden it," and Christian teaching on marriage is lost en route. Furthermore, if what you want done to you becomes the standard, conduct can skid indefinitely downward with the apparent sanction of the Golden Rule. If you don't mind, why should Jones mind?

Or again, there is the question of the limits to which a follower of the Golden Rule would go in doing for others.

Christ has told us elsewhere that we should *love* our neighbors as ourselves, but from the Golden Rule alone you might suppose that the heart need not be involved in our treatment of others. Christ has gone even further and told us we must love others as God loves us. This is the law of charity, which it is impossible to keep without supernatural grace, and which would never be considered an obligation of the Golden Rule taken in isolation.

What it all comes down to is that those who invoked the Golden Rule are decent people (no doubt assails them on this point) and it would be wonderful if everybody were decent. Practical people have no need to ruminate on the matter, and there is certainly nothing to be gained from a lot of ceremonial.

What interests me primarily is the implication that one can live in a Christian manner without believing in Christianity. It is a rather common supposition in one form or another.

"He was one of the three Christian gentlemen I have met in my whole life," I read the other day. The person being praised was an atheist.

"Mrs. X has married out of the Church, but she is the kindest and most generous person on the block."

"Mr. and Mrs. Y are kept from the sacraments by the practice of contraception, but they have a happy marriage and a wonderful home life."

And we know from our experience that the goodness of these people is probably genuine. But doesn't it ruffle our faith a little? Aren't we tempted to think the Church exaggerates a little about the importance of grace? What shall we do?

Shall we close our eyes and our ears and cling to the Faith without thinking? Shall we keep protesting that we don't know all the facts about these people, and maybe give a little sermon about not judging—when all the time we wouldn't have hesitated to proclaim them practically saints on the basis of the same knowledge, plus the assurance that they were practicing Catholics?

We go to too much trouble, when all we need is a little theology.

On the authority of St. Francis de Sales, our last two cases might be examples of "imperfect love." Here are people who have long enjoyed the gift of supernatural charity, probably since childhood. As they have repeatedly acted under the influence of grace there have been built up habits of natural charity, patterns of virtue impressed on their human nature, which do not disappear immediately upon the loss of supernatural charity. We need not hesitate to recognize their goodness for it is real, even though it is not meritorious for them and will not help them save their souls. They both are good, and they are in a deplorable state which needs our prayers.

Now what is true of people is true analogously of societies. The long Ages of Faith built up a reservoir of naturally good habits (institutions) on which Western society has lived for several hundred years. These institutions and traditions had the glow of Christianity about them because they were built up under the influence of grace, and they affected the people who lived by them.

The "Christian gentleman" mentioned above was a doctor, which explains almost everything. All the ideals of our medical profession were the product of Christianity, and when Protestant belief gave way in large areas under the impact of Rationalism, the most idealistic young men (who might otherwise have been ministers, or under happier circumstances, priests or monks) went into medicine.

But the Christian "habits" of society have just about run their course. Almost nothing remains except an aura of common decency. This is what people are really living on when they imagine that it is the Golden Rule.

And however minimal this decency is in comparison with Christian morality, it is still a shade above the ordinary conduct in societies never yet touched by Christ.

31

Star of Wonder
DECEMBER 21, 1958

A T THIS TIME OF THE YEAR THE HARDEN
Planetarium in New York puts on a program of
speculation about the possible nature of the star
which led the Magi to Bethlehem.

The lecturers imply that if there is any truth in St.
Matthew's story of the guiding star, it must rest on some
natural astronomical phenomenon, some unusually bright
astral body which appeared at the time. Maybe it was the
conjunction of Jupiter and Saturn, which occurred in 7
B. C.; maybe it was Halley's comet, which streaked by the
earth in 12 B. C.

Although we are not certain of the exact date of Christ's
birth. 12 B. C. is definitely too early, so Halley's comet is
out. The theory of the conjunction of planets, which has
an interesting history, must be combined with astrologi-
cal symbolism to reconcile it with the Gospel story. Still,
the Magi were astrologers as well as astronomers, so this
supposition can be stretched into the realm of possibility.
There is also the off chance that the star was some other
unusual, but natural astral event of a sort which does not
yield to the backward calculations of astronomers, and
about which contemporary testimony has been lost.

The Church does not rule out the possibility of some
such natural explanation.

Still, the explanation which is most obvious, and which
presents no theoretical difficulties, is that the star was

miraculous. The maker of the universe (and He alone) could easily make a special star for a special purpose, and cause it to operate without interfering with the laws governing other heavenly bodies.

Whichever way God chose to produce that star, it was no mere coincidence that it then appeared, because it was used to direct those sages of Persia to the central event, the focal point, of the whole created universe. It was an event that transcends any in this Age of Space.

When we say that the birth of a Baby in Bethlehem almost 2,000 years ago is the central event of the universe, we mean that it is the most important thing that ever happened or ever will happen, and that it is the reason for the very existence of everything else. This statement demands some theological backing, which will be forthcoming, but first see what is not claimed.

It is not claimed that the Nativity is chronologically or geographically central.

We know from revelation that Christ was born when the time was ripe, but this is not obvious from the study of history, nor will it become apparent now that time has stretched beyond lightyears into new dimensions. All we can know in this life is that the time was ripe because God chose it.

The same sort of thing goes for space. The importance of the Incarnation in no way hinges on the location of Bethlehem. Even though we, with our finite minds, think it fitting for the Central Event to be centrally located, God chose the place for His own reasons: and we know His ways are not our ways.

[The medieval men in the Ages of Faith thought it as natural for the sun to revolve around the earthly abode of divinity as for the central plaza of their cities to open out from their cathedrals. It was upsetting when the Copernican theory decentralized the earth with respect to the solar system. And now we are jarred anew to learn that our solar system is neither centrally located in the universe nor unique, but only one of myriads of others, each containing planets full of unimaginable possibilities for life and events.]

Now let us consider the central importance of the Incarnation. The theology goes like this:

The ultimate reason why anything at all exists outside of God is because God is Good, and goodness is self-diffusive. God did not have to create. Everything created is an expression of this goodness of God. Some things express this goodness in greater degree than others: a tree more than a stone; an act of charity more than a beautiful voice.

The greatest possible communication of God's goodness to the order of creation is that God should somehow unite that order with his divinity. We have an ever-so-faint analogy of this in the value we place on a man's "giving of himself" rather than just giving us something. We would never have been able to guess how God could give "of Himself," until it happened. And even now we do not fully understand the mystery, but we know that One of the Persons of the Trinity formed a bridge between creation and its creator by joining the human and divine natures to one divine person.

This highest conceivable expression of God's goodness was manifested publicly when that Baby was born in Bethlehem, when True God entered the universe as True Man.

That's why the splendor of Christmas is not minimized by the space age.

And let us suppose for a moment that the other planets in space have rational creatures living on them (a possibility for discussion in a future column). If so, then the people on those planets have immortal souls and stand in some sort of moral relationship to God. God has some plan for them which we cannot know from speculating at this distance.

While a multiplication of Incarnations is theoretically possible, we have good reason to believe that the Incarnation of the Son of God is a unique event, the true focus of the entire universe.

So that is why the happenings in that cave in Bethlehem cannot even share their supreme importance with other important events in outer space.

And that is why that Star, whatever it was, has a right to outshine all others.

32

Temperaments and Tranquilizers

DECEMBER 28, 1958

THE GREEKS HAD A THEORY THAT FOUR FLU-
ids (they called them humors)—blood, phlegm, choler
(yellow bile) and melancholy (black bile)—entered
into the bodily constitution and, by their relative proportions, determined the basic dispositions observed among
men. They named these dispositions, or temperaments, after
the predominating fluid: sanguine, phlegmatic, choleric
and melancholic.

Over the ages the Greek classification of temperaments
was a standard guide to self knowledge and the understanding of others. But now modern psychology considers
all this too naive to warrant any attention. The body is not
really made up of these four fluids, is it?

No, it isn't. But temperament is governed by an internal,
diffuse and inherited balance of some sort, and medical
science is rediscovering this in its study of the glandular
systems. The Greek theory was essentially correct, even
if not literally true.

In any case, the descriptive analysis of the four temperaments was based on observation and common sense,
which should carry over into any age. Of course, many
contemporary psychologists consider common sense
"unscientific" and prefer to look for truth in something
they can measure. It is this mania for measurement

which forms the basis of a substitute for classifications of temperament.

You may not find these substitutes very helpful. To use one of them you really should subject your friends to physical examinations so as to carefully record their skeletal structure, the shapes of their heads and so forth. And what will you find out about them? You will find out what type of insanity they would favor if they went off their rockers. Really. The man who thought this system up did his measuring in a mental hospital, and what else could he discover? I'm the leptosomatic, or asthenic type, and I would be a schizophrenic.

Another well known modern classification probably can be worked out with photographs (since it was derived in this way), and if you are careful you can index the degrees of endomorphy, mesomorphy and ectomorphy found in each of your friends. This in turn will yield valuable data about them. For example, you may find out that they have unrestrained voices, or are inclined toward sociability.

So let's return to the Greeks.

I wish I had a lot of space to talk about the Greek classification of temperaments. It has been so derided that it's hard to come by, and the only treatment I know of is translated from German. It's available from the Bruce Publishing Company in Milwaukee for 50 cents. The title is *The Four Temperaments*, and the priest-author, Conrad Hock, writes in the light of spiritual direction. He gives the good and bad points of each temperament and tells of methods of self-training and guidance for each. It's excellent.

Here's a quick run down on them:

If you are the active sort, always wanting to *do* something, you are predominantly choleric or sanguine. The choleric person is a competent, executive type given to impatience, possibly possessed of a nasty temper. And the sanguine individual is a charming optimist who may also be vain, superficial and irresponsible.

But if you just like to sit, you either have tired blood or one of the passive temperaments. Those who sit brooding or thinking profound thoughts, and love funerals, are probably melancholic. And those who both need and are satisfied with the good, earthly things of life, who have difficulty bestirring themselves for an ideal or a cause, are mostly phlegmatic.

Fortunately, because it gives them a certain resilience to life, most people have mixed temperaments. Anyone with exclusively one temperament, no matter which, is out on a limb, and had better send for Father Hock's book right away. These are the people who are "not like everyone else" and never will be. They may be saints or psychopaths or rabble rousers of geniuses or lunatics. It takes knowledge and special effort, and lots of grace to make their lives into something special in the way of achievement instead of specially disastrous.

Actually, one of the effects of supernatural grace is the modification of temperamental disabilities on a profound level. This is the healing aspect of the work of grace in perfecting nature.

Obviously the more support nature gets from natural sources, like a good upbringing at home and an ordered society, the easier it will be for grace. Since even these "normal" supports are frequently lacking today, it is no wonder that so many people suffer from internal instability. Other things being equal, those with temperamental extremes are the first casualties. And beyond a certain point of disturbance, nature is not amenable to the curative effects of grace because of the impediments to its operation which have been generated, and of which must either wear off or be removed.

That is why I, for one, welcome the proper use of the new tranquilizers, anti-depressants and other psychotropic medicines; not just for people in mental hospitals but also for those who are really hard pressed in normal life. I don't understand the biochemistry involved, but obviously these drugs act as temperament modifiers.

One of Pius XII's last allocutions was on the subject of such drugs. He warned against their systematic use to avoid the strains and hardships which are inseparably a part of life in the world, but he said they would provide a valuable relief for many cases, even in ordinary life.

Of course these drugs won't make us saints. But they may help to bring us up to the starting line.

33

Saint Skeffington
JANUARY 4, 1959

THE EMPLOYEES OF THE AMERICAN TOBACCO Company have just donated $1,100 (their office Christmas party money) to the 100 Neediest Cases appeal of the New York Times.* In fact one hears of similar sacrifices daily on the radio since we have, as I wrote, no newspapers in New York.

These sacrifices leave me with very mixed emotions. It is hard to estimate the degree of charity represented in foregoing the [...] removal of office class barriers (paid for by the firm), in order to buy social workers for a spotlighted segment of the population. Still, out of deference to whatever warmth is to be found in the hearts of the givers, and to the needs of a twisted society, I have deliberately postponed airing my views until the money has been duly garnered and distributed.

One thing I am sure of is that the *1M Neediest* appeal is a case study of what's happening to society since the hay-day of the late James Michael Curley,** formerly mayor

---

* In her February 1952 *Integrity* article, Carol Robinson wrote about these cases in which she said: "Every year during Advent the New York Times publishes 'The 100 Neediest Cases,' capsule case histories from the files of the private welfare agencies. The public is invited to contribute funds for the relief of the unfortunates, which it generously does — this year to the extent of about $300,000." (Also found in her collected *Integrity* articles which we published in *Thy Faith Hath Made Thee Whole*, 412)
** James Michael Curley (1874-1958), mayor of Boston from 1914-1955, governor of Massachusetts from 1935-1937.

of Boston, and now immortalized in *The Last Hurrah.**
James Michael Curley had virtues as well as charm, but he
was so unmistakably careless about other people's money
that he was often censured by responsible citizens, and
even served time in prison for his faults.

That was in the old days. The fact that Curley now seems
to have had a heart of pure gold (in the order of mag-
nanimity, not avarice), I attribute to the drastic interim
changes in society. Paradoxically, the very thing which
destroyed his political career (the coming of the welfare
state) has led to his canonization in the popular mind.

Sometimes in reading the *Neediest Cases* I am myself
tempted to promote his Cause. If he had known old couples
who were slowly starving to death on their social security
allotment, he would never have sent a social worker "to
help them manage their limited income."

It was after the Great Depression, when James Michael
Curley was falling out with Franklin Delano Roosevelt, that
the needs of the poor grew far beyond the assuaging power
of political bosses and private charity. The government had
to step in and feed people with public funds. It is difficult
to know whether this could have been done simply on an
emergency basis. But in any case, the government is now
permanently saddled with what used to be known as the
corporal works of mercy.

This shift from private to public responsibility relieved
private charitable organizations of their chief function: to

---

* Wikipedia does an excellent job of summarizing the movie: "*The
Last Hurrah* is a 1958 American political satire film adaptation of the 1956
novel *The Last Hurrah* by Edwin O'Connor. It was directed by John Ford
and stars Spencer Tracy as a veteran mayor preparing for yet another
election campaign.... The film tells the story of Frank Skeffington, a
sentimental but iron-fisted Irish American who is the powerful mayor
of an unnamed New England city. As his nephew, Adam Caulfield, follows one last no-holds-barred mayoral campaign, Skeffington and his
top strategist, John Gorman, use whatever means necessary to defeat
a candidate backed by civic leaders such as banker Norman Cass and
newspaper editor Amos Force, the mayor's dedicated foes."

distribute the largesse of the rich to the deserving poor. However, they still had endowments, and what is more they had trained personnel (the New York School of Social Work had recently discovered the rich resources of Freud and the Case History Approach). To put it briefly and crudely, the welfare workers in these agencies became the recipients rather than the channels of philanthropy, and started building up their elaborate works of supererogation.

It is for these private agencies that the Times makes its appeal in New York, and I think there is a similar appeal in all our large cities.

For years I suspected that the public hadn't fully grasped the change in society but thought that their contributions were going for medical expenses, rent, food or some other primary need, even though a careful reading of the cases would have disabused them. Perhaps many people did complain about being duped, because this year the Times carried a special statement by the Commissioners of Public Welfare on the indispensability of private welfare.

Nevertheless the cases are written in such a way as to arouse our compassion for the very real needs which are admittedly being taken care of by the welfare state. The often dubious, and never bleeding, need for the guidance, counseling and supervising of the Social worker is mentioned unobtrusively.

In fact, I counted five or six cases in which the need for the services of a social worker was resoundingly nonexistent.

At the opposite extreme there were about the same number of cases which needed this sort of help by anyone's standards. These cases concerned families so essentially and permanently defective as to be virtual wards of society. Caring for them is more a matter of accompanying their children to juvenile court, or arranging to institutionalize this one or that, than of any high-toned counseling. And it seems to me that this is the social worker's most legitimate field of operation. The work is dreary, but it has meaning. These people are the inevitable casualties of a society which wisely places a higher value on the right to marry and to propagate than on eugenics.

The nameless and faceless people of the majority of the 100 cases are, however, rootless moderns more or less like ourselves, though less fortunate and perhaps a little less well fortified with physical and mental strength. Most of them would never have bogged down at all if they could only have had a vacation in time, or a couple of extra dollars, or the helping of a neighbor, or (as I very much suspect) a deep faith and the consolations of religion.

Even after they have cracked under too much strain nobody is disposed to give them a vacation. Instead of two weeks on a Florida beach, away from all their troubles, with nothing to do but rest, and with the sun to renew their courage, they get (of course) "the guidance and help of a counselor in overcoming their problems."

And finally there are many, many cases of that curious sort of meddling which measures so clearly the enormous gulf separating the welfare state world from the normal but destitute world of James Michael Curley. The social worker is always getting in between a situation and its proper solution, or explaining an explanation, or easing people into the inevitable (without religion), or pointing out the obvious.

If a baby needs parents it must first be placed in a foster home so the social worker can work with the foster mother to quiet the baby's fears and build up its sense of security, and only then can it be uprooted again for adoption.

1959

34

Just Heat and Serve

JANUARY 11, 1959

T HE SUPERMARKETS IN THE NEW JERSEY SUB-
urbs are much grander than those on the New York
side of the river. I do believe that the one I visited
recently had a bin of frozen prepared foods stretching
thirty feet, and it included semi-gourmet concoctions put
up by one of the better New York restaurants.

If I had been going directly home I would have laid
in a small supply, because I had already been softened
up by an article about how good these frozen dinners
are, how cheap they have become, and how silly it seems
not to succumb to their convenience. Not quite so good
as a home cooked meal perhaps—but think of the time
you save.

The only strange thing about this episode is *me*. I'm not
the last person who would ever stoop to a TV dinner, but
one of the last. In my case it is a question of principle,
not of delicate taste buds.

Anyhow, since I was so tempted, and because the year's
end is a natural time for reviewing the past, I am moved
to bring up to date the state of my thinking on "progress,"
as represented by the TV dinner.

In my experience there is a very considerable minority
of citizens who greet each new simplifier, or time saver,
or by-passer of the human brain, or substitute for human
skill, or chemical replacement of the organic, or excuse for
taking it easy, with loud groans and ineffectual protests.

Over the years these few dissenters have prophesied that we would all die of arsenic poisoning (from chemical fertilizers), that our children would become astigmatic and bird-brained (from watching TV), that our teeth would rot (from eating white sugar and store bought bread), and that the human race would fall below the level of primitive man in survival skills (from the disappearance of craftsmanship).

As I have said, and as everyone can see for himself by looking around, especially in supermarkets, these maledictions have gone unheeded by those in the mainstream of our country's life. The majority of Americans move into split-level housing developments without guilt-feelings; nay, with rejoicing. The lush colored advertisements of *Life* and *The Ladies' Home Journal* do not fill them with horror. These ads are simply a faithful reflection of what they themselves eat and wear and do, of their own family ideals and sense of values.

Or perhaps it is the other way around; the advertisements show the people how to live and they learn to measure up within the next few weeks. In any case there exists a close harmony here which makes the negators of progress look like the lunatic fringe of the most triumphant society ever.

"Crackpots," they are usually called.

In retrospect, crackpots they often were, and are. They have started cults based on nature mysticisms (which sometimes gave way to orgiastic rites). They have pranced about nude in colonies, or flexed their muscles endlessly. Again and again they have isolated themselves to develop a new primitivism. Or they have simply become cranks who are always writing to the newspapers, or never cutting their hair, or going around barefoot or living on strange diets.

I wonder if these crackpots would also have been outsiders in a wholesome society? Possibly not. Many of them have a hold of real truth but have no framework into which it will fit, so they exaggerate it and go off to build their own framework, with its altar to the wheat germ.

The irony of the situation is that *balance* and *wholeness* are practically the creeds of crackpots, and yet they find themselves unbalanced and in schism.

I find myself less and less patient with people who are fanatical on the subject of denatured food but who never think to say their prayers. To be more afraid of getting cancer than of going to Hell is a worse sort of aberration than the one they are fighting.

But much is possible in the way of reform where contempt of progress is combined with and subordinate to a spiritual objective. The primacy of the spiritual distinguishes the holy fool, like Gandhi, from the genuine crackpot; the Trappists from the cultists.

I guess those of us who make minor efforts to restore God's world to God and who see the implications of the TV dinner, have to feel their way along the compromise road. We should be willing to suffer the martyrdom of premature dentures and the ignominy of vitamin pills if that is the lot of our generation—but not as a result of walking down Easy Street to the Leisure State.

35

Obiter Dicther

JANUARY 18, 1959

ABOUT HALFWAY BETWEEN OUR HOUSE AND the Harmon Station where my husband takes his commuting train, is a driveway leading to a high hill over the Hudson, and on its gatepost this sign: Institute of Motivational Research.

"What's that?" our friends usually ask.

"Never mind," we tell them, "you'll be happier not knowing."

Some of them decline to be shielded from even the most unpleasant facts of life. So we explain that this is the very site where Madison Avenue wedded Freud, and that there are swarms of the most forward looking people up there analyzing why you buy things. You, meaning our guests.

We count ourselves out, for we have long since lost our innocence and our pliability. In a supermarket I am thoroughly atypical. I close my eyes and grope, or I choose the brand recommended by my mother-in-law. Sometimes in desperation I test the veracity of the TV ads, but no more than once. If I'm not completely satisfied I don't send back the unused remainder for a refund, I simply abandon the product and all the other products of the same manufacturer. And I warn my friends, when I think of it, to do likewise.

I have illusions and weaknesses, but not the sort catered to by the Institute of Motivational Research.

They think I do everything for emotional reasons, probably subconscious, to which they hold the key. If I feed my husband liver and spinach, I'm expressing marital hostility. When he smokes he's thumb-sucking by way of a socially acceptable substitute. Eating soup is clearly retrogression, but we don't do that very often.

As for cars, there is scarcely a make now which hasn't been designed under the eagle eyes of people like those in the Institute, as a mobile symbol of our frustrated desires for virility or the admiration of the neighbors. You wondered why they are so odd looking? That's it. It's the emotional catharsis that counts. Unfortunately all this is lost on me because all cars look pretty much alike to my undiscerning eye, and I can't judge their vintage within about ten years.

When we buy a car we look for something that will start in the winter and that is less in excess of what we can afford than other cars. And you will understand why we don't try to impress our neighbors when I tell you that the nearest one to the East is Jackie Gleason and that the whole area is pretty toney.*

All in all, remote as we Robinsons are from the practice of the Beatitudes, we have been touched by the Christian message, and it has left us immune to the Institute of Motivational Research.

The man who heads this august institution is a Viennese psychologist named Dr. Dicther. Naturally he is surrounded by a corps of trained research workers, probably with Ph.D.'s. In bad weather I see them abandoning their cars at the gate (mostly the trim, Volkswagen type, indicating their efficient preoccupation with higher things) to negotiate the hill on foot.

Dr. Dichter charges $500 an hour to confer with company executives and advertising magnates on the proper merchandising of their products. Here I must caution my readers that sums paid for such services have a certain prestige value, like painted neckties. But the money doesn't

---

* toney: marked by an aristocratic or high-toned manner

come out of the pocket of anyone present at the conference. By devious routes we all are paying for it. You needn't fret, though. Otherwise this money would go to the government for taxes, which might be preferable, but still is not a spotless repository in these bureaucratic days.

I suspect that the learned Doctor doesn't profit much himself. That looks like a drafty old house up there and those trained researchers cost money. He'll probably wind up poor and unhonored, which I expect will prove a chastening experience.

He will be followed by someone worse, of course, with yet more hideous ideas, who will lead the huckstering business down the next steep grade.

I wonder why I'm telling you all this, when we have been at such pains to spare our guests.

You don't need me to introduce you to Dr. Dichter's manipulation techniques, which you can't escape so long as you have any money to spend. His influence is blowing down your neck as you ask for Gleem because you can't brush your teeth after every meal (over which you have long been guilt-ridden without realizing it). He is chalking up another victory for "Psychological Obsolescence" at your first vague discontent with last year's automatic washer, the one with only three and not five control buttons.

Well, so long as you are being manipulated, and now that you know by whom, I may as well give you my six point program for the retention of Christian dignity under the duress of neo-paganism:

1. Never let anyone call us Consumers. We are temples of the Holy Ghost.
2. We buy food and clothing because God has given us bodies (now hallowed by His Presence) which need these things.
3. We are under no obligation whatever to keep the economy going by purchasing a surfeit of goods. If it's that kind of economy, let it fall.

4. As a matter of fact, we are under the opposite obligation—to be frugal—not wasteful, not extravagant, and we must not choke ourselves and our families with the goods of this world.

5. We ought to keep measuring our shopping lists against the spirit of poverty.

6. Let us avoid occasions of sin. Above all, let us never wander aimlessly through the aisles of stores, where mountains of impulse-buying merchandise lie in wait to snare us.

36

Thoughts on Christian Unity

JANUARY 25, 1959

S INCE THIS IS THE TIME OF YEAR THAT PUBLIC efforts are made to put a friendly face on religious differences, it will be useful to take a look at how matters stand.

In my opinion the Protestant-Catholic antagonism has about run its course. There remains much latent ill-feeling among sincere Protestants, but this stems mostly from inherited prejudice and misunderstanding stimulated by a few noisy Catholic haters like Paul Blanshard.

Even these attacks support the theory that the long "protest" is over, for they are not centered on theological matters, nor do they usually charge Catholicism with religious abuses such as really were provocative causes of the Reformation. Instead the Church is accused of seeking political power and inhibiting the liberties of democratic citizens. Most of the accusations are not true (and will be dispelled by the evidence of events even if people will not listen to their refutation), or they are true but are misrepresented as evil. Although Mr. Blanshard speaks as a Protestant, he does not speak for Protestantism and he seems to appeal especially to those nominal non-church-going Protestants, educated to scepticism, whose liberal views are far more secular than religious.

Let's put it this way: anti-Catholicism is not enough to make a Protestant, you also have to be a Christian.

When people who call themselves Protestant are strongly anti-Catholic, it is well to examine their positive beliefs. If they do not believe in the divinity of Christ, and if all their so-called Christian efforts are solely for the betterment of society and humanity in this life without supernatural reference, they are gravitating, willingly or not, toward the atheistic-secular synthesis, and their enmity should not be attributed to our separated Christian brethren.

In one respect of course, Protestantism is inherently anti-Catholic, because it was a break with, and a recessive movement away from, the Church. But the recession ended some time in the recent past (largely from having spent its force) and with it ended the original anti-Catholic momentum. The long war is over and most of the survivors do not even know how it began.

Increasingly today both sides are disposed to examine the Christian rather than the protesting side of Protestantism. Here lies the great basis for the reunion of Christendom, the fact that a union of some sort still survives, however attenuated. We all look to Christ as our Redeemer, though with every degree of belief, from a living infused faith down to dead faith, acquired faith and even grace-given searchings for faith.

At some indiscernible point there is a shadowy line which separates those who approach the fullness of faith from a minimal point, and those who decline to raise their sights above the natural and human in their search for good. Christ would have these outsiders also in His fold, but theirs will not be the path of the reunion of the churches.

Reunion does not mean some sort of peace treaty based on the status quo. (Brotherhood Week is something like this, though on an even broader basis. In effect, it may sacrifice truth to good fellowship.)

Neither does reunion mean the unconditional surrender of the Protestants to the Catholics. Unity is a matter of One Faith, and Faith is a supernatural gift which we can neither coerce not manipulate. (That's why the Church Unity Octave is so excellent. It recognizes different degrees of separation from the fullness of Faith, and that the work of unification is primarily God's.)

It seems as though God in His Wisdom will draw many more men to Himself along their familiar Protestant paths before there ceases to be a divided Christendom.

Meanwhile the walls of unfamiliarity and strangeness are crumbling on both sides.

Within Protestantism there is a great ferment which on the whole is an effort to regain a fuller Christianity. It does not yet aim at Catholicism, but at the restoration of post Reformation losses; a fuller liturgy, more orthodox theology, and the reunion of Protestant churches.

However, the nearer Protestantism gets to its own roots the closer it will be to Catholicism in doctrine and in practice. In fact the Lutheran Church in America, which is having a tremendous boom, admits itself closer to Catholicism than to the rest of Protestantism, simply because as a national (German) church it was isolated and remained unchanged.

Even more striking, though different, changes are taking place in the Catholic Church, it is as though she was paralyzed exteriorly by the long and bitter siege, and now she is making in a few years the adaptation which would otherwise have taken place gradually over centuries. She is shedding her medieval garb, taking on a new simplicity, bringing everything up to date and restoring the practice of some of those aspects of Christian life which she restrained for so long in order to guard against Protestant exaggerations.

So as the Protestants approach us, we will look more and more inviting. And in my view it is wise not to interfere with the trend toward rapprochement by emphasizing or unduly discussing doctrinal differences. Prayer, yes. Quiet explanation, yes. But how many firmly held are the differences which on the surface seem so great? And are not Protestants themselves in the process of re-examining their tenets?

Let's save our critical zeal for the insidious doctrines of secularism, which daily grow in strength and which are the common future enemy of all Christians.

37

Ethics and Morals
FEBRUARY 1, 1959

THERE WAS A RADIO SHOW THE OTHER DAY (which I did not see and which I deplore, but am not at the moment bent on deploring) about prostitution and big business. Among the people present and commenting were the New York Commissioner of Correction (a woman) and a Jesuit priest. She said that the ethics of our present society is a poor one; he spoke about *immoral* conduct and its effect on the whole moral fabric of business.

It is the choice of words which interests me. Watch and see how carefully people other than the avowedly religious today avoid using the word "morality." They go out of their way to use the Greek equivalent, as a deliberate rejection of what they consider to be authoritarianism in matters of conduct. When a recent letter of the President of Wellesley to the alumni spoke of promoting "high ethical conduct" among the students, I took this (rightly I think) to mean that Wellesley officially disavows the canons of revealed religion.

There should be no conflict of teaching between ethics (as the philosophy of good conduct) and morality (as God's revealed rules), but today these two words symbolize two worlds. Even though the Greek is still sometimes used legitimately and harmlessly, especially when referring to professional ethics, still one must realize that the choice of the word "ethics" usually sets man-made against God-given standards.

People who talk about ethics want to be good on their own terms. They want to decide themselves what is right, and they don't like to have their conduct pinned to God, to rewards hereafter, to an authoritative Church, or even to absolutes like the nature of human nature. Usually they find some shifting sand or other, like expediency or pragmatism or "the greatest good for the greatest number."

I once went to a funeral at the Ethical Cultural Society in New York. There was no corpse, as the body of the deceased had quietly and unceremoniously been cremated the night before. There was, however, a eulogy, which began by stating clearly that the bereaved could have no hope of reunion with the departed, and went on to describe the life of a kind, generous, urbane, cultured humanitarian who was good to his family, loved by his friends, and tireless in promoting social causes. He was probably the Ethical Culture Society's Exhibit A, proof to them of man's ability to stand on his own feet.

I thought of him the other day when I was reading Saint John of the Cross. Saint John points out how we must desire God, our supernatural goal, with our whole hearts, and that the desire for any temporal or natural good whatever, if not subordinated absolutely to God, darkens and wearies and weakens our souls. He says we can experience this ourselves everytime we prefer anything to God. And then he goes on to say that there are certain people who do not experience it because, since they do not walk in God, they are unable to perceive that which hinders them from approaching Him.

Here I put the "ethical people." Because they aren't walking in God or toward God, they are blind to what hinders them and others from reaching God.

It so happens (and not by accident) that these "ethical people" are quite preoccupied with social causes and social welfare, which is their frame of reference for doing good. Here their blindness is frequently apparent.

Earlier this year I examined the "100 Neediest Cases" presented annually for our compassion. As the material needs of these people had already been aided by public welfare, the healing of their other ailments (loneliness, domestic strife, misunderstandings, etc.) was to fall to social workers.

In not a single case were these disorders ascribed to a disharmony of the soul with God's plan for it. I thought a lot about this, because resistance to God's plan (whether by sin, or the pride of insubordination, or by worldly desires) is a paramount factor in my experience and in the lives of the people I know.

Many of the Neediest must also be floundering in the consequences of their rebellion or divided desires, in spiritual torment which calls for spiritual treatment.

Most social workers are too blind to see this, either because they themselves do not walk in God, or because they operate by professional techniques which exclude spiritual factors. They consider it "unprofessional" for instance, to speak of conduct as good or bad (which has a moral connotation). One must use terms like positive or negative, which refer to man or society by implication.

Ethical people are not to be confused with sinners. Sinners do evil according to God's standards, whereas ethical men do good according to their own measure.

But let us not for a minute doubt whether the publican or the Pharisee does more harm.

The whole history of socialism demonstrates that it is an effort to supplant God's plan by one of human devising. It was deliberately atheistic in the beginning. It is triumphantly atheistic in its terminal synthesis, which is Communism. In America we have thousands upon thousands of intellectuals who unwarily fall into the Marxist trap of socialism by an unwitting and pharisaical adoption of the so-called "ethical" standards inherent in irreligious relativism.

38

Suggestions for Lent
FEBRUARY 8, 1959

W E GET A FIGHTING CHANCE TO PREPARE for Easter, which is more than can be said for Christmas.

We don't have to buy all those presents and send out all those cards, so if we can resist preoccupation with our Easter outfits we can concentrate on polishing up our souls.

My first suggestion is that we ignore all efforts to turn Easter into a fashion parade. Let's not fight it; let's just quietly resist it in our own lives.

There are various ways of doing this. What's essential is to stay out of the stores. One way is to skip the whole business of new clothes, which you probably don't need any more than I do. Alternate courses are (1) for Southerners, buy new spring clothes before Ash Wednesday; (2) for Northerners, buy them after Easter, which is early this year anyhow, and it probably will be snowing.

The next thing is to work up a proper attitude.

I don't think there is anything wrong with approaching Lent as though it were spring training or a series of sessions at the local Slenderella, though on the spiritual plane. We are somewhat flabby and overweight in our souls, and never mind how grim it is going to be, we hope to come out changed for the better, maybe transformed into deeper and more purposeful Christians who will stop drifting through life in the familiar rut. We can make a mental picture of ourselves before, and dream about how lovely we will emerge after some six weeks of unremitting effort.

Never mind that this approach has nothing directly to do with Christ's death and resurrection. By the time we get to Good Friday we'll have cleared the way for a new appreciation of the central mystery of our faith.

So let's suppose that we see Lent as a regime for our soul's health. Now we can brief ourselves on the Bishop's regulations for fasting and abstinence. Although these sometimes seem to get more and more complicated, they do not put much of a burden on us any more. (The first year I was a Catholic they were stricter and I was of the strict observance and I almost fainted everyday before lunch). Anyhow, we are urged to supplement this modest mortification with special efforts of our own.

Here is where I think we would do well to avoid stressing old favorites, such as giving up smoking or candy or desserts. I know there are a lot of people who wait for this season to air out their lungs or bring down their blood pressure. There are also many who used to be able to forego these things, but can't any longer. Cigarettes, especially, are a great attachment, but that does not mean they are a great evil, and while we tilt with them annually (to win temporary skirmishes or surrender ignominiously), our souls are being encompassed by enemies of far greater magnitude.

Maybe it would be a good idea to moderate these indulgences by rationing them carefully. A common mistake is to suppose that these preliminary dragons must be slain before we can go on to greater spiritual battles, and this is not necessarily true. As a matter of fact it is often easier to slay them after we have brought other aspects of our life into line. With most people these are not vices of intemperance so much as conditioned reactions to the pace and din and nervous tension of our times. They seem to symbolize a way of living which we really reject in our hearts.

I suggest that instead of concentrating on the old favorites we give up worldliness. I don't so much mean "I-love-the-world" worldliness, which most of us don't have; rather, "the-world-is-too-much-with-us" worldliness. Its chief features are muchness, noise, crowds, talk, activity, curiosity and rapid change.

The chief antidotes to this sort of worldliness are silence, solitude and simplicity. Let's work on them.

The restoration of silence is a project for strong men. Maybe the television set could be put in the garage. That radio that's always turned on (whether in the car or in the house) but which no one is precisely listening to (just a noise to stave off thought), could be doused. But the effect won't be complete unless the movies, the cheap magazines, the comic books (this for the kids— buy them a box of candy and a book about the saints) and other escape distractions are also firmly banished.

Silence is quite a shock at first and rather terrifying. Still, the average family should be able to get through to about the First Sunday of Lent on the momentum of their initial resolutions. After that we can begin to fill the silence with all those quiet sounds which formerly got lost in the din: family Bible reading, Lives of the Saints, some liturgical practices, family prayers, even conversation.

Silence will bring quite a bit of solitude along with it. It will be a relief to be alone with the family, without having Bob Hope or Jack Paar or Groucho Marx visiting. But it will be good to get away from the family too, to be alone with God, either behind closed doors or in church.

And finally there is simplicity, but that shouldn't be hard.

I see the practice of simplicity as the habit of choosing what is opposed to the complexity and confusion of the world. For instance, walk instead of ride wherever possible— not because walking is hard, but because it's slow. Cook instead of opening cans, or bake bread at home, because this culinary effort represents the return to an

older and more wholesome atmosphere. And so it goes —
make music rather than turning it on, play games instead
of watching them.

There is one more suggestion, but you will get it from
everyone because it is so important: go to Mass and Com-
munion every day if possible.

All these suggestions of mine are only directed toward
making a clear open space in our souls, so the grace of
the Sacraments will have a better chance to make us new.

39

Why Johnny Can't Think

FEBRUARY 15, 1959

I T HAPPENED AGAIN THE OTHER DAY. A YOUNG lad assured me his teacher was more concerned that he learn to *think* than that he acquire a body of knowledge.

So I put him through some simple tests — why this or why that, or what do you think this word might mean? They were exercises which would give no trouble, even to a simple person with a clear and inquiring mind. They were questions a thinker would probably ask himself.

This lad has an excellent IQ, but it turned out he really couldn't think at all. He seemed to have a mental block. His face was pained, worried and tense. His brain was obviously racing here and there in search of clues from the storehouse of his memory. He made some random, unrelated guesses. But he didn't even begin to reason "Let's see ... if this, then perhaps that" or "it has to be A or B ..."

I know just how this is, because I went through the same thing.

"Never mind what you learn, we're going to teach you how to think" is, of course, the same theme song of "liberal" education. Roughly translated it means "we don't care whether you are nourished or not, so long as you learn to chew."

The reason such educators say it is more important to chew than to eat is, of course, because they haven't any food. They pretend that's not important and make a lot of snide remarks about those who stuff food down students' throats without letting them get their teeth into it. The people who do this stuffing are all the people who have something to feed their pupils. The liberals label them dogmatists. It is intimated that a claim to the possession of Truth guarantees that it will be furtively inserted into the gullets of the young, as though it were stolen goods in the first place.

There might be some hope for students if they really did learn to chew, because they could forage around for food later. Instead they are only taught to suck in air. To understand how this works, we must first be clear about what thinking is.

Thinking is a process by which Truth (food) is brought to bear on date or situation. There are three factors: the beginning truths, which are principle or universal laws — and always general; the observed date, which are always particulars and which in themselves are meaningless; and the conclusions or applications, derivative truths which follow automatically if you reason properly.

The problem we are considering arises because men came to believe it impossible to arrive at the beginning truths. They reached this point gradually. First they denied revealed Truth (which is where the first principles of theology come from) and then they went on to doubt the natural capacity of the intellect itself. After a long series of heresies and philosophical errors, it got so that men declined to consider even the possibility of finding the universal truth which starts the thinking process.

But they still had minds and they still had a thirst for Truth, with which we all come equipped, so they lunged into the second factor. They went on fact-finding binges. They accumulated mountains of data. They sent sociological and anthropological expeditions to far corners and near nooks and crannies. But of course bulk does not give meaning to what contains no meaning in itself. And furthermore, you cannot approach the accumulation of factual data without some reason for asking this question instead of that one.

As an example, the case histories of social workers and the elaborate questionnaires of psychologists never ask if a person is baptized, but always inquire into sexual experience.

To put it briefly, somewhere in the course of this fact finding mania, some kinds of "first truth" or basic premises are surreptitiously supplied by prejudice or emotion, or they are even taken for granted because they are what everyone thinks at the moment. But they are never clearly stated and defended. Most "intellectuals" even imagine that they are deriving these premises directly from the data.

Take the late Professor Kinsey, for instance. Ostensibly he was just making surveys of sexual *conduct*, but actually he concluded to sexual *standards*, or rather to the impossibility of standards. He did this by *assuming* that what men do is a reflection of what they ought to do, but of course he never held this assumption up for discussion or debate; he covered it with the smoke screen of his lurid case histories.

Take another case. A sociologist makes a "survey" of tenement families in a certain area and finds out that they have more children than their wages can feed and their apartments accommodate. What right has he to conclude that they ought to practice birth control? Why doesn't he conclude that they should be given higher wages and bigger apartments? His conclusion depends on his clandestine first premise, but he would have us think that it grew out of his statistics.

And another. The psychologists who spy on small children through those glass walls that are transparent in only one direction take it for granted (why?) that human nature is most clearly revealed (and so studied) when it is still below the level of the reason which characterizes it.

Which is like holding that you can learn more about oaks from acorns than from the trees, or about Christianity from the record of its early years than from the contemporary living Church, or more about society from primitive tribes than from great civilizations.

Poor Johnny. He will ding his freshman college sociology text four inches thick, bursting with statistical data, and almost 100 per cent atheistic in its "derived" principles. After he has been thoroughly trained to suck in air he will be the creature of the propagandists for the rest of his subrational life. They need only feed his blocked brain plausible explanations with an emotional appeal. Johnny will operate by conditioned reflexes rather than by reflection — because Johnny has never learned to think.

40

Suffer Children
to Be Little

FEBRUARY 22, 1959

ISN'T IT ODD, WHEN YOU THINK OF IT, THAT the age of reason is determined by moral responsibility and not by some intellectual virtuosity. Even sanity is judged the same way. We don't ask a person pleading lunacy if he can play a good game of chess; we try to find out if he knows the good and bad of his own conduct.

Near here there is a Montessori school where children learn to read at about three and a half, write, multiply and do many other things before they are six. These are ordinary children, with an exceptional opportunity to learn; not prodigies and geniuses who conduct orchestras or write Latin poetry during their most tender years.

Yet none of these feats of learning indicates that the child can distinguish between right and wrong and thus make the choice between God and sin which marks his arrival at the age of reason. It's true that some children do attain the use of reason very early (St. Thérèse reached it at three), but this is a spiritual precocity or a special grace. Most reach it at about seven.

In order to make a moral choice, more than just physical growth is necessary. A child needs to have an informed conscience, to know what is good and what is wrong. He also needs good dispositions and a will that has, through training and discipline, gained some control over the actions of his body.

Some children are so neglected that their little bodies grow wild. They can see and taste and touch and hear, but more or less like little animals. They respond to impulses, threats and appetites, but their minds remain untaught and their wills undeveloped, and they cannot easily attain reason in this condition.

Spoiled children have a hard time too, even when they have religious instruction. Everyone conspires in the corruption of their wills, which follow after their senses in search of self-gratification. Under such circumstances it becomes exceedingly difficult to recognize and choose a moral good, and even harder to carry the choice into action.

Some benighted souls think spoiled children are lucky, because they "have everything," but there is another class of children whose misfortune goes unnoticed by quite serious and respectable people. These are the children who are carefully brought up in every respect except one: they are given no religious or moral training. Otherwise they are carefully trained and disciplined. They learn to appreciate good music, to use their bodies rhythmically, to eat regular and wholesome food, and to love beauty. But nothing is said to them about God, or about what is good or bad. These are the children who seem so attractive in an all-American way. They are clean and well-dressed, well-mannered and full of enjoyment of the good things in their young lives, but curiously dull.

It's hard to believe that these children don't quickly reach the age of reason, and maybe some of them do because their souls are operating in spite of their parents. Yet the multiple disasters which have happened to some of our most attractive young people would seem to indicate the contrary.

Youngsters who are ill-prepared or unprepared to cross the bridge of reason, have blighted childhoods and, if we believe the psychiatrists, can remain infantile far into their adult years, failing in one life situation after another.

Naturally they love Peter Pan, but James Barrie has misrepresented the case for perpetual childhood. A reluctance to grow up is not a sign that childhood has been too blissful to part with. A good childhood serves its purpose and is outgrown. The Peter Pans among us still hanker for childhood because in one way or another it has been denied them.

Real childhood is an age of innocence which can truly give us an inkling of that spiritual childhood toward which we are to grow. In it children come to the age of reason knowing about God, loving Him, and full of the desire to be good. Then follow those plateau years of peaceful growth on a child-like pattern. A child is docile and trusting. He is unconcerned and usually oblivious of the great problems and upheavals of the adult world which surrounds him. He is anxious to be helpful; he responds readily to incentives and praise.

Compared to others, Catholics do a creditable job of bringing children across the threshold of reason and into the golden years of childhood. Yet eight or ten years later these same children can be the most difficult of teenagers and the despair of their parents. Why?

There are surely a number of reasons, but the one I want to consider at the moment is the invasion of adult (not even adolescent) troubles and teachings and manners into the child's world.

This takes many forms: letting children watch adult programs on TV, hiding nothing from them in the way of domestic troubles and problems, exploiting their views on matters beyond their ken, cloaking them in premature sophistications, and slanting their studies to the current scene.

There is also something quite inappropriate in the present tendency to interlude the courses in our parochial grade and junior high schools with considerations of the vast controversies in the field of Social Justice. Important as these may be, glib answers to thorny questions of integration, foreign aid and right-to-work laws belong in the realm of propaganda and cannot be adequately assessed by the young people I am talking about. It is as though they were being taught the last and latest and most ephemeral things during the one period in their lives when they are really ripe for a remote and deep and comprehensive view of the world into which they have so recently come.

No wonder they turn out to be smart alecs, if the world is so stupid as to care about their sixth grade opinions on public housing. If they had been feeding instead on the classics, they might be a little more humble. And how will they achieve any spiritual depth if they think that the perfect practice of Christianity is symbolized by living next door to Negroes? They would do much better to cultivate a devotion to an exemplary Negro Saint, the Blessed Martin de Porres.

41

The Neutral Zone
MARCH 1, 1959

A SOCIAL WORKER HAS WRITTEN OBJECTING to my criticism of the non-moral terminology used in his profession. I choose to make his answer public because it is an important point and he represents the popular professional view.

My original remarks were apropos of the *100 Neediest Cases*, short case histories published at Christmas time in New York to raise money for social workers to supply the non-material needs (usually guidance in some form) of unfortunate people whose corporal needs are met by public funds. In none of these 100 Cases were domestic or personal difficulties traced to spiritual causes — sin, resistance to grace, materialism, or indifference to God and His plan.

I pointed out that in my experience difficulties of this sort often had spiritual roots, and consequently were subject to spiritual cures. However, the way the social workers write case histories, there is no hint that religion or morality or grace are relevant to the sordid parade of human misery. One gets the impression that the 100 Neediest are a race apart; pathetic, victimized people quite unlike you and me and our neighbors, who are all sinners and who bring most of our troubles on ourselves.

My critic took the general and familiar line that I am pointing a finger of accusation at these poor people, that I have no right to judge them, and that I am ready to throw stones at fallen women.

But I'm not. What I'm really trying to do is to bring these people back into the human race, from which they are isolated by the curious techniques and barbarous language of social work.

My chief objection to the techniques and language is that they are calculated *neutral*, and since life is not neutral, they falsify it.

For instance, guilt is always a feeling. My critic himself used the expression "guilt feelings." Now I don't deny that one can feel guilty, and very unpleasant it is. But why do we never hear from social workers about remorse of conscience, which is usually the core of the trouble, to which such feelings are simply peripheral misery? Is it because the word "conscience" brings in concepts of good and bad and sin, and the whole moral law and God, and the big question of how to get rid of sins?

Feelings are safer because they are below the level of rationality and moral responsibility. If guilt can be kept on that level it never need be brought to the moral tribunal. Instead it can be handled psychologically, which means endless talk with someone trained in what my critic calls the "democratic principles of acceptance, non-judgmental attitudes and client self determination."

[Obviously, there are those who suffer abnormally from "guilt feelings"; they are not the guilty or the conscience-stricken, and they need psychiatric assistance.]

My critic traces these principles to our social heritage in Judaeo-Christian culture. I don't know what is "democratic" about them or why the adjective "democratic" is expected to add lustre to anything in the way of a principle, but let's skip that for a moment.

What is this principle of *acceptance*? I mean, since it is a great principle in the Judaeo-Christian culture, what is the Judaeo-Christian name for it? I suppose it means in practice that no matter what the client has done you won't tell him it's wrong, and you won't throw him off the relief rolls (or you wouldn't if you still had control of the relief rolls) or you won't treat him like a leper. Acceptance is obviously not Christian charity, because it falls so far short of the full meaning of charity.

You might say it is a little like one of the effects of charity, for charity falls on the deserving and the undeserving, the good and the bad. But charity is love. It has a warmth not suggested by the word acceptance. And charity is intrinsically related to God, for it is a gift from Him, and it loves Him first and others in Him and for His sake. So I give up. I can't exactly place "acceptance" in the Judaeo-Christian culture.

However, I do know what "non-judgmental attitudes" are. According to the literature I've read, this expression means avoiding moral judgments. Here again I have difficulty placing this principle in the Judaeo-Christian tradition, in spite of my correspondent's reminder about the woman taken in adultery. After all, it was adultery, and when Our Lord told her to go and sin no more He was judging adultery to be a sin. That's the sort of judgment that social workers and psychologists are reluctant to make. They will even talk about certain sexual deviations without any reference to the fact that they are morally evil.

What Our Lord said about the woman taken in adultery was that He didn't condemn her, and it is in this sense that we are not to judge our neighbors. We do not know their hearts, so we can't judge their intentions, but we sometimes cannot help seeing their wrong acts, and social workers let themselves in for a torrent of information about wayward humanity. Let them at least keep their moral bearings.

That brings us to "client self determination" where the only puzzle is why this expression is preferred to "free will" or "freedom," as the case may be.

It's hard sometimes not to mock the high flown language of the social sciences. But I don't mean to mock here, because I don't think it's funny.

"Whom the gods would destroy, they first make mad."

As I see this question of "neutral" language, it is a way of first making us mad, in order later to destroy us. It takes us out of the moral-theological framework of the Judaeo-Christian tradition, so that we can afterwards be moved into the new atheistic synthesis with its rigid standards based on secular absolutism.

Perhaps one should say: "Whom the Devil would destroy, he first confuses."

42

Poverty of Spirit
MARCH 8, 1959

DO YOU REMEMBER O. HENRY'S STORY ABOUT
the poor man who pretended he was rich one day
every year? For 364 days he lived a colorless existence in a cheap furnished room, so that on the 365th he
could pose as a gentleman of wealth for one evening.

I used to think that was wonderful. Here was a man who
passed up the small comforts of a barren and sordid existence for an annual taste of beauty and the finer things in
life! As a matter of fact, there might have been something
mildly heroic about it if the values had not been all wrong.

For they were wrong. He was not selling everything to
purchase the pearl of great price. He was a man with the
spirit of luxury, who used calculated means to indulge
it in the only way possible for those low-salaried times.
His spirit was that of the American Way of Life, but his
opportunities were severely limited.

Over the years I've seen that same spirit repeatedly, and
it has now become a national trait. It was first noticeable
among secretaries whose office wardrobes ate up most of
their earnings, but gave them a superficial appearance
which was a clever facsimile of the best dressed women
in the world. Most of them returned at night to tenements
in the uglier parts of Brooklyn or Jersey City: the parental roof of careworn and anything but chic mothers; of
short-sleeved fathers who had in their time fed six kids,
on half of what the secretaries were earning.

Among men the disparity centers around expense accounts. As hotels and the Pullman Company have learned, no male dining on the firm or the government ever chooses the Blueplate Special. It's always shrimp cocktail and steak, even though he settles for hamburger and crying babies at home.

It seemed as though there was no one who did not reach for his moment of deceptive glory. Even the young Harlem hoodlums managed very temporary possession of violet colored Cadillacs.

Finally we all got to live like kings, or the American version of kings, so far as clothes and gadgets and food and cars and houses were concerned, and this is our present condition. The hidden unbalance is credit, or installment buying or unpaid bills.

Furthermore, we can truthfully say to anyone who demurs, that we now have very little choice in the matter of how we live. Most people don't even remember that there used to be poor (not destitute, not profligate, not alien-minority) people who lived decently and frugally and unpretentiously for generations according to the pattern of poverty.

How would one dress as a poor man now? Where would you find modest but adequate low cost housing? How would you get around without a car? How could you keep your job if you were conspicuously different from your coworkers? In brief, how does a Christian now practice the spirit of poverty?

As I see it, the spirit of poverty lies in a desire to be poor, just as the spirit of luxury is a hankering after actual luxury. Neither is necessarily realized in practice, but only because of external impediments such as the duties of one's state in life.

Nobody wants to be poor, nor would be poor if he could, except out of a preference and love for spiritual things: freedom, contemplation, the pursuit of wisdom or the desire to imitate Christ.

I was poor once, though not painfully, and for mixed motives which included a degree of necessity. My fifth floor tenement apartment had three rooms, heat, hot water, a river view if you twisted your head out the window, and cost $24.50 a month. You can't find places like that anymore.

One night I had a visit from an elevator operator (not in our building of course!) who was soliciting votes for a Marxist-minded political candidate named Marcantonio,* In the course of our conversation, my caller pointed to the Royal York Apartments (doormen, Muzak in the corridors, complete air conditioning, three rooms for $250) which were nearing completion in the next lot where the gas tanks used to be.

"Wouldn't you like to live there"? he demanded.

It seems that Marcantonio was aiming to get us all in apartments of that sort.

At that moment (for I wouldn't have liked it) I saw the great abyss that separates Christians from Communists, and remembered with appreciation Eric Gill's assertion that Christ came to make the rich poor and the poor holy.

Ever since then I've known that we Christians and the Socialists ought to be moving in opposite directions, in spite of the fleeting common causes we find in the field of social justice.

We *ought* to be going in different directions, but in fact we are not noticeably doing so.

And the direction we are going in is theirs, not ours.

---

* Vito Anthony Marcantonio (1902–1954), lawyer and politician who served in East Harlem for seven terms in the House of Representatives.

43

On Digging Your Own Grave

MARCH 15, 1959

SOME YEARS AGO[*] I HELPED START A MAGA-zine called *Integrity* which had its first headquarters in a former coal bin on New York's East Side.

Before we were even settled we had a visit from a man in the protection business. There were, he said, a great many incidents of vandalism in the neighborhood. The shop of the Hungarian dressmaker opposite had twice been broken into during the night. And for a small monthly sum he and his men would undertake to see that nothing similar happened to us.

Naive as we otherwise were, we realized he was offering to protect us from himself, in the characteristic manner of gangsters.

I thought again of our little encounter with organized crime while reading *The Black Book on Red China*[**] on how the Peking government deals with religion. The Communists simply offer the churches protection from themselves, for a consideration.

Of course the Communists make no attempt to conceal their atheism, whereas our gangsters put up a token pretense of benevolence, which they probably would drop if they were a little more sure of their power.

---

[*]   Founded in 1946.
[**]   Edward Hunter, *The Black Book on Red China: The Continuing Revolt*, New York: The Bookmailer, 1958

But the deal is fundamentally the same in both cases: you can be destroyed now — or gradually. If you refuse our demands we will destroy you; what we are demanding is the power to destroy you when we wish, and in return we will wait to do so until we have squeezed you dry and you have dug your own grave.

Both types of bandits have everything to gain if you stall for time. The Communists intend the eventual destruction of all religion, but meanwhile they would like to have religious authority use its prestige to shepherd people into the Marxist fold. Gangsters want to milk the profits of a going business. You will have to pay them more and more tribute as their power to substitute for the law increases, and of course this power is increased every time you or another small businessman kicks in and keeps his mouth shut. It is of no direct financial help to the gangsters if you go out of business, but they will see that you do if that is necessary to maintain the prestige of their threats against the other businessmen in the neighborhood.

The only big decision you have to make is whether or not to accept their protection and put yourself in their power.

In China that meant first the deportation of all foreign missionaries and the cutting off of all funds from outside. Then the Protestant seminaries were consolidated into one large training center under the control of Communist puppets. The churches had to make a common front with the new government, promoting patriotism for Socialist China. They had to justify their continued existence by tangible results in the increased productivity and docility of Christians.

It was harder to sever the Catholics from outside protection and allegiance, but the Peking government has finally succeeded in establishing a schismatic hierarchy which will continue to administer the sacraments while promoting the atheistic government which will one day cut it off entirely.

It is important to see that yielding is not compromise, but collaboration. It is not a matter of giving up some things in order to retain others. No, it means lending active support to the enemy, whether fostering lawlessness or promoting atheism.

Of course it is easy to talk about these things so long as we are not subject to hideous pressure ourselves, but still we may be subject to them some day and clear thinking is a sort of preparation.

The big temptation must lie in the time factor, since the businessman knows that he's acting against the interests of all honest business when he pays tribute, just as the church-man knows that he has nothing to hope for in the long run from an intrinsically atheistic regime. But anything can happen, can't it, given a few days or weeks or years?

Yes, there's always the long-range possibility of rescue by police reform or legislative investigation, or by the forces of Chiang Kai Shek or the United Nations.

So stalling might be an admirable tactic if only the price weren't collaboration. There is nothing to be gained by saving your business for a little while, only to lose it and your honor. Or to postpone the death of the body by forfeiting the soul also.

Someone once told me of a German school teacher who wanted to quit her job when she was first conscious of Nazi pressures on her classroom work. She was advised to remain "so as not to leave her young charges totally at the mercy of Hitler's doctrines." She did, and every day she got deeper involved as a Nazi tool, until she committed suicide.

Now to get back to our visitor—.

In retrospect, I see that we gave him the only possible answer. We said thanks but we are already protected, and pointed to a Sacred Heart badge fixed over the door by a previous tenant. He left, and left us alone.

So we really were protected. In this case God seems to have used a superstitious fear of religion, common among gangsters, as His shielding right arm. In China He often uses death (of which the Communists are the unwitting agents while He supplies the requisite courage by His grace) as protection against Hell.

44

People and Population
MARCH 22, 1959

T *HE READER'S DIGEST* WRITES ITS SHORT BIOG-
raphies to formula. The noble hero or heroine, devoid
of personal faults, or even traits, is moved by pity to
start a reform or a movement, preferably single handedly,
and finally succeeds against great odds.

Into this mold the *Digest* poured Margaret Sanger's life
some years ago, and produced the very image given out for
public adulation by the Planned Parenthood organization,
of which she is the figurehead and American foundress.

We see her as an earnest upstate girl who came to
New York as a public health nurse just after the turn of
the century. Overcome by compassion for the poor slum
mothers with their chain pregnancies and dire poverty,
she began her long fight to legalize the dissemination of
birth control information and instruction. It was a very
uphill fight of course, and she was even jailed once, but
she won through and is now basking in the success of
her movement and the honor everywhere accorded the
mother foundress.

As a matter of studiously omitted fact, the young Margaret Sanger was quite an odd ball. Before she began her
fight she went to England and studied under Havelock
Ellis, whose monumental opus on sex was long banned
as obscene.

Although among Mrs. Sanger's written works is a book
called *Happiness in Marriage*, she and her husband lived

in separate apartments and made dates with each other. No doubt this arrangement was in accordance with the nonsensical ideas of the emancipated women of her time, but then, so was the idea of birth control. If the thing to be feared about marriage is a common life, why shouldn't fruitfulness be the thing to be feared about sex?

I thought Mrs. Sanger a pathetic old woman when she appeared on Mike Wallace's program last year. She didn't look like an ogre, but she seemed restless and terribly deficient in some quality that I couldn't immediately identify.

Dorothy Day of the Catholic Worker was interviewed on the same program at about the same time. She had just been released from The Women's House of Detention where she had served a month for refusing to take shelter in an air raid drill. It was when I contrasted these two women, both of whom had had the courage to suffer imprisonment for the causes in which they believed, that I realized what I missed in Mrs. Sanger was the dignity and peace which comes from a deep spirituality.

The last thing I intend is to anticipate God's judgment of Margaret Sanger; what I really want to do is to shake loose some of the sentimentality which clouds the judgment of Christians about Planned Parenthood. One way to do this is to show the clay feet of its prophets.

Dr. Marie Stopes, who was Margaret Sanger's opposite number in the English birth control movement, died last year at 76. When I was in college her name was bantered around in fun because of a book she had written called *Married Love*, which was also banned as obscene, and which eventually sold a million copies.

After reading Dr. Stopes' obituary in the *Times* I felt the poor woman never really had a chance. Her father was an anthropologist; she herself was a biologist and paleo-botanist, with a doctoral degree in Science from the University of London and one in Philosophy from the University of Munich. In other words, she was mired up to her ears in 19th century atheistic rationalism.

She wrote poetry and children's stories. She had wanted four children of her own, but a severe accident prevented her having more than two, and of these two, one died in infancy. In the Movement her emphasis was scientific and eugenic. She took a strong moralistic stand against smoking, which seems silly, but after all she had been robbed of better causes.

Our next character is Jawaharlal Nehru, Prime Minister of India. Last month his country played host to the International Conference on Planned Parenthood.

Nehru is the great apostle of peaceful coexistence. When he took over the Indian government he set out deliberately to make India a Socialist state, but by democratic methods; so he is the person to watch if you like the aims of Communism (which are the same as those of Socialism) but you deplore the violence of Soviet Russia. You will learn from his experience that force is a necessary means for achieving these identical aims, and so you may be persuaded to take another good long look at the aims themselves.

At the Delhi Conference, both Nehru and the Planned Parenthood people showed their hand on the question of compulsion. Nehru admitted that although Family Planning had been the official policy in India for 8 years, the results had not been encouraging. His Congress party had already voted to find drastic measures to curb the rise in population. They were looking for a pill which could be in everyone's food and would have the effect of reducing fertility, but this had not worked out, so they intended to set up hospitals for the sterilization of males. The operation would be performed free on those who came voluntarily.

This did not scandalize the Planned Parenthood organization, and why should it have? They also had delegations from Japan (where graphic information about artificial contraception is displayed everywhere, and abortion is legal and available) and from Communist China (which is estimated to have reduced its numbers by about 50 million in the last few years using the most direct of all methods — murder).

While the delegates piously voted to ask the U.N. to declare it a basic human right to obtain family planning information and use it, they were actually plotting to do away with the age-old human right to *have* children.

And this brings us to our last character: James A. Pike, Protestant Episcopal Bishop of California.

On Bishop Pike's return from last year's Lambeth Conference, he stated categorically that it was a matter of Christian duty, apparently under pain of sin, to practice family limitation.

Now we've gone full circle. Men started by thinking they had more pity than God and that they knew better than God how to run the world. Why shouldn't they end up telling God what's right and wrong?

45

What's in a Name?
MARCH 29, 1959

I N 1942 THE BIRTH CONTROL FEDERATION IN
America was renamed the Planned Parenthood Federation, in accordance with the modern belief that a
change in name can make an odious thing smell more
like a rose.

It is neither here nor there, but interesting that the new
name was first suggested by Anne Fremantle,* who has
since become a Catholic and a prominent Catholic writer.

"Birth Control" suggests a prejudice against babies and
the use of contraception. "Planned Parenthood" suggests
conveniently spaced offspring whom one can afford to
send to college; so it seems to smell quite a bit like a rose,
especially now that we know about the rhythm method of
spacing babies and because its clinics take pride in actually
helping apparently barren couples to conceive. While Birth
Control looked much like sin in the service of selfishness,
Planned Parenthood looks like science and benevolence
cooperating for greater human happiness.

It is my present purpose to destroy this roseate illusion.

This could easily be done by haranguing about the mon-
strous evil currently done or countenanced by the Planned
Parenthood organization, but the reader might then conclude that the people involved were a lot of hypocrites,

---

* Anne Fremantle (1909-2002) was an English American journalist, translator, poet, novelist and biographer. She converted to the
Catholic Faith in 1942.

which most of them are not; or that the evil is somehow
accidental, which it is not.

So let us open our eyes to the fact that it is almost
always under the pretext of bettering society that we are
today led down the garden path, and that the invitation
is usually given in the name of Planning.

The first thing to grasp is the new use of the word Plan.
It no longer denotes just an orderly way of accomplishing
something, like a Christmas Savings Plan. Today's Plan
spells out Utopia. It is a shining social goal which will be
achieved by the determined and calculated application of
social and scientific techniques. It doesn't grow organically
the way a medieval town developed, nor is it the sum
total of persevering effort, in the way that fifty cents a
week means $26.00 plus interest next December first. It
needs planners who work out the blueprints, and then a
transcendent effort or force, by which they materialize.

Now what's wrong with Planning, even if it is Utopian?
Let me start with an illustration.

Some years ago a new mother, someone dear to me,
pointedly assured me that her infant daughter was a *wanted*
child. I knew that the mother was a big wheel in the state
Planned Parenthood association, and she knew I was a
convert to Catholicism; still her remark was curious. Could
she have thought that unplanned babies are normally
greeted with distaste? Surely not.

After long thought I realized that she meant to disparage babies who were *welcomed* (as gifts of God, or even of
nature) by contrast with those duly ordered and delivered.

This reminded me of the advice that used to be given
to the parents of adopted children, and probably still is.
When it came time to tell Sonny that he was adopted, they
were to reassure him by pointing out that natural parents
have to take what they get, but we *chose* you.

Of course they didn't choose him, some social worker
did, but it is interesting to note the implication that they

might have been stuck with a terrible lemon if they had used the ordinary channels of family increment.

I hope you begin to see that the Plan is really a substitute plan.

The original plan is Providence, which is God's scheme for running the world. Having babies is a key point in this original plan, because we are an animal species which consists of a multitude of individuals born in time. But because we are also rational, the use of sex, which is what sparks our biological fertility, is supposed to be controlled by reason. So God set up the family as the basic unit of society; marriage as monogamous and indissoluble for the sake of child rearing. This structure was supported by a considerable part of the moral law, which in turn was long supported by the positive law.

Every time the word Plan is used in its new sense you will find the Socialist mentality at work, even though sometimes only faintly or unconsciously.

This is true of Planned Parenthood, which is concerned with only one facet, but an important one, of the new Utopia—population control. For these people the fear of statistics replaces the fear of God. They are becoming hysterical about the geometrically soaring world population. By the yardstick of mathematical calculation the year 2000 will find the earth overcrowded and this will drastically reduce the standard of living.

If we look at this possibility of a serious reduction in the standard of living through Christian eyes we will miss its crucial significance to the Socialist. He plans to make all of us happy by an arrangement of society which will fulfil all our material desires. If population growth threatens this indispensable prerequisite to happiness (as so curiously many things do), then by fair means or foul, which is to say by persuasion or violence, our numbers must be lopped off. You will recognize this as the global version of the old argument about having fewer children so you can give them more.

It is characteristic that Planned Parenthood prefers to calculate on the basis of statistics, which is a social science or tool thereof, rather than to take a good look at some political considerations which pose an opposite sort of threat to the growth of the species.

We must realize that the substitute plan cannot take over until people have been divorced from God's plan and that in the free countries of the West this divorce cannot be accomplished by direct force.

Thus it is that every weapon of persuasion and propaganda is being used to destroy or pervert the residual Christian conscience. So far as I can see, this has been eminently successful in the field of Birth Control.

The Catholic Church now stands absolutely alone among our religious bodies in defense of God's order with respect to the use of sex. So standing, she is beginning to lose battle after battle in her fight to hold our American laws to the laws of God.

Is it possible to exaggerate the seriousness of the threat that this situation poses in the battle of the Marxists for the American mind?

46

The Fixed Point

APRIL 12, 1959

"THE FUTURE," SAYS THE CHURCH TO THE MAN and woman who are about to be joined indissolubly in marriage ". . . is hidden from your eyes...not knowing what is before you, you take each other for better or for worse, for richer or for poorer, in sickness and in health, until death."

It may look as though they are about to step into an abyss of uncertainty. As the Church sees it they are about to embark on a sure path. "Henceforth you belong entirely to each other..." Through life they have a fixed point by which to steer their course, and this fixed point is for each of them the other one, with all the duties and responsibilities which are entailed, and with what crosses and pleasures come their way. They may or may not be happy in this life, but they have security; there is always that same other person in terms of whom each has the necessity of working out his salvation.

Those who get divorced and married again never have this security. Often the second marriage, or even the third, is more suitable and happy than the first, which may have been contracted hastily in wartime, or to get away from home, or while too immature to make a proper selection. But such a happy marriage rests on its happiness rather than on a bond which cannot be broken. So even if the happiness is enduring, it leads them nowhere. Their life is a brief moment of joy in a garden on which the sun will soon set; it is not a journey. Instead of security, they have a fleeting possession of happiness.

But life is by its nature a journey, not a pool of pleasure. That is why security is a path and not a possession. It is a right road, not a bulletproof vest or the guarantees of a Welfare State. We know the rightness of that road by a fixed point, and that fixed point is often a person.

Here we have a key to much of the contemporary mis-understanding about security. Here we also have the key to certain neglected virtues, notably fidelity, loyalty, patri-otism, obedience and honor. They are the habits by which we adhere to the fixed points, as by fidelity husband and wife adhere to each other.

What is true of marriage is true of all the other aspects of life and, in a special all-encompassing way, of the life of the soul.

In our journey to Heaven, Christ is our Way, our fixed point—as He Himself has told us. It is only by supernat-ural grace that we can get there, and this grace is God by created participation. So by the Divine Life we are drawn to union with the Divine. If we lose this fixed point, either as a goal or as a means, we lose all our temporal bearings too, and as a consequence all things begin to betray us, because we have betrayed Him.

It works the other way, too. If we return to Christ as our end and means, we get the power to rebuild or discern our temporal roads.

Take the case of children, whose fixed point is obedience to, and respect for, their parents.

I know a 14-year-old girl who left home as the culmina-tion of a prolonged rebellion against parental authority. There was nothing wrong with her father and mother except inadequacy. They belonged to the generation which bene-fited from the last remnants of our Christian capital, but so feebly that they couldn't transmit it further. There was noth-ing wrong with the daughter either, except inchoate rage.

She went to live with the family of a young Episcopalian minister and there, in the course of a year or so, she received a Christian orientation which transformed her life. Then she came home of her own accord, full of respect and obedience for her parents because she was observing the Fourth Commandment. Once afterwards she said to her mother: "I see a lot of things wrong with you, but I won't mention them because you are my mother."

She was a lucky teenager. Our public schools are trying to help teenagers by encouraging them to violate the Fourth Commandment. Essays are assigned on such subjects as "My father's word fault." There are classroom discussions of parental decisions on dating. Individual grievances are openly aired. If parents are not respected because they are parents, then it is natural, after they get used to the idea, for children to sit in judgment upon them. And of course the next step down is for children to betray their parents in the name of some arbitrary or forced loyalty.

Wei Kuo-chu, a member of the Youth League and a student at the Shih tung High School of Shanghai was (according to a Peking paper of August 6th, 1955) cited and congratulated for having denounced his father, Wei Chih-Ying, as a counter-revolutionary.

What honor is to parents, patriotism is to one's own country: a primary loyalty and gratitude based on natural circumstance and serving as a fixed point for the lives of citizens.

So fighting against loyalty oaths is like fighting against parental authority, and all this talk about not liking the *methods or the manners* of those who try to protect our internal security is a little like objecting that the man who is saving your mother's life is unrefined.

Either we are patriotic or we are not. And if we are, we love and protect our country in spite of her imperfections, and in spite of ours.

The American soldiers who were captured in Korea had a very bad record for patriotism. Many of them compromised with the enemy, in spite of the fact that they were not subjected to force or even brainwashing. The enemy began the way the school teachers begin, by airing the weaknesses (some true, some not) of the United States, as though the soldiers were bound to love and respect their native land only when she deserved it in their eyes.

Our army has since revised and strengthened its instructions for behavior under captivity. However, the alarming fact is that we were not able to presuppose the virtue of patriotism, and slight changes in training are not going to build it.

The future for all of us, as for the bride and groom, lies hidden from our eyes. Instead of trembling with fear, or clutching at this or that vain protection, it would be a good idea to look for the fixed points.

47

Liberals and Conservatives
APRIL 19, 1959

M Y WORKING DEFINITION OF A LIBERAL IS:
One who does not see a danger until it is too late
to do anything about it.

It is an outrageous definition, of course, and purely negative. It omits to mention what liberals work for; it bypasses their virtues. One might as well define Achilles by his heel.

Still, I find it useful for reconciling the harm that is currently being done in the name of Liberalism with the manifest good will of most liberals. To be specific, this definition explains to me how liberals can hate Communism while strewing roses in its path.

It enables me, for instance, to contemplate Adlai Stevenson with equanimity while thanking God that he is not our president. Mr. Stevenson visited Soviet Russia in 1926 and again recently. He is pleased with the new atmosphere. He finds a less desperate ideological intensity (N. B., liberals generally shy away from intensity about ideas); more preoccupation with industrial development. All of this indicates that we can hope for the best, etc.

"Don't get excited," I say to myself. "Don't wonder if he's ever bothered to dip into the torrent of literature which exposes the true nature of the Communist plot. Of course he has, but what's that compared to his personal observations and the optimistic tendencies of his own nature? He's a liberal and that explains everything."

Senator Humphrey is another case. When he suggests that instead of racing Russia in building stockpiles of nuclear bombs, we fight side by side with her against our common enemy, cancer — I no longer ask myself if I have heard right. I know I have. I do not even wonder if the Senator has all his marbles, that he should advise solving a political crisis by ducking it. He has his marbles, it's just that he's a liberal.

It seems to me that these examples demonstrate the chief debility of our contemporary liberals: they are congenitally incapable of viewing the evils of our time in a clear light, and with a steady hatred.

Liberalism attracts men of a certain natural bent, or disposition. If we didn't have the labels "Liberal" and "Conservative" we would still have the opposing human tendencies which gave rise to them; and these polar attractions would be discernable in all men, though more decisively in some than in others. We can therefore assume that there is, or ought to be, a complementary benefit from this dichotomy; just as there is from the division of the species into men and women.

The havoc arises, as it does in the case of the sexes, when one element tries to fulfil the function nature has allotted to the other.

Now my analysis is that liberals tend to be short sighted by contrast with those of a "conservative" disposition. Put it this way: they can't see the woods for the trees. It therefore follows that they should let the conservatives handle forest fires, while they deal with nearer, and if you like, nicer arboreal matters.

That phrase about seeing "the evils of our time in a clear light and with a steady hatred" was lifted from Monsignor Knox's panegyric for Hilaire Belloc, who is a good example of the conservative temper, either alone or in contrast to his friend, Chesterton.

Somewhere in his letters Belloc speaks of the loneliness and estrangement suffered by men who have a penetrating view of the truth. They see what other men do not see, and since it is often an unpleasant truth or a threatening danger, they must try to communicate it to an unwilling audience. They must try to save people from what seem to be non-existent perils.

The conservative type of mind can be found among quite simple people. There it often seems like stubbornness. A man without education may one day find a truth profound enough to explain his life and innermost concerns. He will cling to it, mull it over, love it and defend it; and it will somehow set him apart from the fellowship and enjoyment of his companions.

But in educated and more intelligent men, the conservative tendency is clearly linked with a power to see, more deeply than others, the implications of principles and the consequences of radical actions.

William F. Buckley, Jr., in a recent television interview, pointed out that our American minds are already largely formed in the Marxist ideology. The realization that we already think, extensively but unconsciously, like Communists, is no news to a conservative. But it is certainly not obvious to the majority of Americans, who are under the intellectual domination of the liberals, a domination exercised through liberal control of newspapers, magazines, radio and TV and the educational establishment of the entire nation.

The man who is temperamentally conservative is forewarned in principle when significant events take place, because he is able to discern the involvement of a principle long before others.

The myopic individual must wait until extreme consequences are realized before he perceives an evil. It's something like military strategy: an army can be disposed in such a way that victory is virtually certain, though the fighting has not yet begun.

I remember it was on a certain specific day that my father (a Cassandra-like conservative) foresaw Hitler would take over all of Germany. I had never heard of Hitler but I mentioned it to a school friend, who told her father, a man of German ancestry and a liberal, who in turn ridiculed my father's fears. My father and men like him also warned of the 1929 stock market crash and they were laughed at.

Of course conservatives make mistakes like all human beings. Sometimes they see two Communists under every bed, whereas there is really only one. Our family ate Campbell's tomato soup until it came out of our ears, all because my father had laid in a giant supply against some evil day or other that didn't arrive.

Some Conservatives have great all-around powers, but frequently their energies are totally concentrated in their long range vision. They live by the mind and their intelligence is neither clouded nor warmed much by the heart. That is why they are so often inept, awkward and uncomprehending with respect to the art of living, which is the liberal bailiwick. Even Belloc was half envious of Chesterton's universal popularity.

www.ingramcontent.com/pod-product-compliance
Lightning Source LLC
Chambersburg PA
CBHW021631120626
46545CB00002B/490